CW01496873

FROM THUNDERBIRDS
TO PTERODACTYLS

FROM THUNDERBIRDS TO PTERODACTYLS

SHANE RIMMER
My Autobiography

Dear Kieron and Annetta

May the winds blow softly to you

love Shane & Sheila

SIGNUM BOOKS

To our grandchildren,
Ella, Hugo and Kit

First published in Great Britain in 2010 by Signum Books
an imprint of
Flashpoint Media Ltd
22 Signet Court
Cambridge
CB5 8LA

© Shane Rimmer 2010
Shane Rimmer has asserted his right to be identified as the author of this work,
in accordance with the Copyright, Designs and Patents Act, 1988.

All rights reserved. No part of this publication may be reproduced, in any form
or by any means, without permission from the publisher.

A CIP catalogue record for this book is available from the British Library.

ISBN 978 0 9566534 0 6

Edited by Marcus Hearn
Designed by Chris Bentley
Cover design by Damian Rimmer

Printed and bound by Replika Press Pvt Ltd, Kundli, Sonepat (Haryana), India.

Contents

Acknowledgements

Thanks to my son Damian, who pitched himself unreservedly into the illustrative beginnings of the book and corrected my meandering ways at the word processor with a patience and stoicism I had never given him credit for.

To Chris Bentley, for so much in the way of ready encouragement, finding the inside track and always picking up the phone.

To Tony Barwick, friend and fellow golfer, who taught me how to become a fellow writer.

To my wife's brother Dr Dave Logan, who has piped over the most practical kinds of medical advice from his gulf-side home in Florida.

Eleanor Currie in her Toronto studio, who gave me my first inklings of what singing was all about.

Kees Blokker, for building such an impressive website and keeping it so nicely in tune over the past years.

Gerry Anderson, for harnessing me into Thunderbird 1 and then plotting some out-of-this-world flight patterns.

The Fanderson bunch – generous, always a pleasure to meet and intensely loyal.

To my sister Noreen, for letting me out of the upstairs cupboard she locked me into when I was seven and she had just turned five.

To Sheila, who has put it all together and given us a life that has been so lovingly worthwhile.

Foreword

Going back many years, I was preparing to film a new television series to be called *Thunderbirds*. It was to be the most expensive and ambitious TV series I had ever undertaken and I wanted it to be my very best show. It was to be made using very sophisticated puppets that we had developed over a number of years, and the puppet workshop was busy designing and making the puppet characters. Although I say it myself, the new puppets were probably some of the best of their kind in the world at that time. Overhead, our brilliant puppeteers were ace at controlling their puppets on the end of very fine control wires painted to match the backgrounds, making the wires almost invisible.

The one problem we couldn't overcome was that the characters couldn't express any emotion. How could they? Their faces were made of rigid plastic.

We interviewed a large number of actors and I selected a young Canadian called Shane Rimmer to voice the puppet of Scott Tracy, one of the most important characters in the whole show – after all, he was the guy who was to head up all the rescues. Shane transformed Scott the puppet into Scott the romantic heroic lead in the series. Shane was, by virtue of his brilliant voice performance, able to make Scott Tracy spring into life.

Looking back, it was quite remarkable that after a few episodes had been aired Scott Tracy became a big hit with the young females in the vast audiences the series attracted. Even some 40-odd years later some women still remember their love affair with Scott in their younger days. Shane deserved his success for he was and still is a great actor.

But there is more to Shane than his magic achievement of turning a puppet into flesh and blood. It wasn't done with smoke and mirrors, it was achieved by Shane's remarkable skill and professionalism.

Gerry Anderson MBE

Chapter One

Time and place: an early March morning in 1963 on a misty south-west drive out of London, on the A316 dual carriageway.

It was the first day's call for four edgy young actors who'd been chosen by Stanley Kubrick to play the air crew in a film that would take cinema audiences around the world on a bizarre roller-coaster – *Dr Strangelove*.

At the moment we were missing a navigator – civilian name, James Earl Jones, already drawing thumbs-up notices in both Hollywood and New York. He was probably just now touching down at Heathrow Airport in answer to Kubrick's call to play the fifth member of the air crew.

Here on the A3 the ground mist was starting to unfurl. I glanced over at the large mileage board coming up on the left – Shepperton, five miles.

Not far – getting closer. Calm down.

I was driving the car for the very good reason that I was the only one of us who owned one – a 1950s Opel, which two days before had taken me, my luggage and seven litres of oil from Frankfurt am Main into the west end of London. The oil just managed to keep the engine turning over until I got to my repair garage with maybe three drops to spare. They poured in another dollop of lubricant, patted me on the head, and got me back on the road.

The reason for the frantic dash was a phone call from my agent to the continent, where I was on a cabaret tour of France and Germany for the American Air Forces club circuit in Europe.

'They called! He wants you!'

'Who's they – who's he?'

"They' is the casting department – the 'he' is Stanley Kubrick!'

'You're kidding!'

'You know that recorded interview they took of you?'

'Sure I do – but I thought it was a wash out.'

'No – he liked it – thinks you'd really fit in well.'

'You know what? I can't remember the name of the film.'

'You ready? *Dr Strangelove or: How I Learned To Stop Worrying and Love the Bomb.*'

'Are you serious?'

'Yes! Peter Sellers is in the main role and it's crammed with big names ... George C Scott, Sterling Hayden ... Keenan Wynn.'

'When?'

'Two day's time – and early! I've been trying to get a hold of you.'

'Sorry, I've been moving around a little.'

'Okay – just get back here. I'll try to get you a good fee!'

'Don't worry – I'll do it for coffee money.'

'Easy! And listen – there are three others who could do with a ride.'

'Tell 'em to call me when I get back home – I'm out of here.'

Back on the near-empty A316 – the interior dialogue was down to a trickle which made the engine bump and grind more like a tumble dryer than ever.

'Man, your engine sounds like a tumble dryer.'

I exchanged glances with Frank Berry, a fellow Canadian in the seat alongside.

'Yeah, just what I was thinking.'

I'd hardly known him before this morning – he referred to himself as a sleight-of-hand comic and magician but never got around to explaining what exactly that was. He was quietly shuffling a deck of cards that were probably marked. I wasn't sure what his acting background was, as if it mattered, but his audition patter apparently had Kubrick in stitches. We could do with a little of it about now.

'Anybody got any lines?' a mournful voice asked from the back seat.

The voice belonged to Paul Tamarin, the third member of the crew. We'd nicknamed him Igor because of his Bolshevik bloodline. I answered him over my shoulder.

'I think today is just a 'look and see day' – to get acquainted with the bomber and everything.'

Frank added, 'And to meet Stanley Kubrick.'

'I hope I don't get stuck for something to say,' Igor commented.

'You?' Frank answered. 'Never.'

Igor was a lean, crew-cut 23-year-old who now hailed from the Bronx, New York, by way of the family birthplace in Leningrad. He'd been telling us in detail how, pushed by family and friends, he'd struggled for ten years to be a child prodigy but didn't quite get there under the age limit. So he'd traded in his fiddle for a one-way ticket to London and a film career, during most of which he'd been playing suspect Russian emigrés.

'Life's a puzzle, Igor.'

'What about Sleeping Beauty here?'

Igor pointed to the figure of Glen Beck in the corner of the rear seat. He hadn't been saying much on the way, which wasn't surprising as he'd fallen asleep with his head swivelling against the window. Minutes away from his date with destiny, how could he do it?

'Better wake him up so he can remember his name.'

So there we were just trying to get ourselves present and accounted for and then some 20 feet ahead was the gated entry road to Shepperton Studios. We followed it around to the right, brushing past a tight cordon of privet bushes, and pulled up at the Security Gate. Alongside was a long, low, flat-topped building with a large 'check-in' wicket and a uniformed Commissionaire sitting very much alert at the desk behind it.

The Commissionaire first looked at the car and the wisp of steam sneaking out from somewhere under the bonnet and then at the four of us inside. For a moment he appeared a little reluctant to come any closer. But he did, although not too close.

'Mornin' boys, congratulations for making it here – can I have your names?'

We sounded them out and he checked them against what looked like a long list.

'Ah, seeing Stanley, are you?'

It would have to be Igor who answered, wouldn't it?

'Yeah, that's right … ol' Stanley!'

'All right, lads. Take a left at that first corner and it's straight down from there to 'A' Stage. That's where you'll find the man. There should be someone there to look after you … okay?'

He was already lifting the desk phone, probably to report that the awkward squad had just pulled in. I was turning back to the wheel when he finished the call, put down the phone and gave a thumbs-up out the window.

'Good luck to you, boys,' he called.

As we started away, Frank waved back then turned around to us, nudging me on the elbow.

'That was really a great kind of a welcome, wasn't it?'

I was half way into the left-hand turn, just avoiding an oncoming low-loader piled with enough concrete slabs to sink London Bridge.

'I hope it'll still be like that tomorrow.'

The road straightened and, in a moment, led us into the studio proper. We passed through a random sprawl of shooting stages, cutting rooms, carpentry workshops, tech labs and storage areas for everything from dismantled film sets to rows of stand-up Klieg lights, generators and hundreds of feet of coiled-up cable lengths. 'A' Stage was such a colossal size it came close to blocking out the horizon for a minute. We rounded the next corner and saw a young member of the crew dressed in jeans and windcheater, posted at the front of a closed green door and motioning us to stop. A naked red light beamed some two feet above his head.

'Hi guys! You can put it over there.'

He pointed to an empty place along the wall where we could park, then motioned me to cut the engine.

'Sorry, they're doing a bit of a 'ssshhh' scene with Sterling Hayden and those mikes in there pick up everything.'

We exited the car on tip-toe and trooped over.

He examined us a little soberly and then broke into a wide smile.

'Hey, really nice to see you, fellas – you're all the bomber crew, right? I'm Ben – Third Assistant. Better give me your names so I can introduce you to the AD.'

He must have caught the slight confusion spreading across our faces.

'You know, Stanley's assistant director – his name's Greg.'

We managed a kind of collective nod and repeated our names for the second time that morning just as a bell sounded from behind the green door and the outside red light blinked off, signalling the 'all clear'.

'Okay, we can go in now and you'll meet Stanley.'

A loaded glare from the three of us muted any kind of reply from Igor.

We formed up and followed Ben down a lengthy breezeblock corridor, then, after a quick left, into the *Dr Strangelove* sound stage. Why they call it a sound stage I'll never know, because all you're ever cautioned to do is keep quiet! But it was almost impossible to keep back a gasp at what we'd stepped into.

The first sight was overpowering, like stepping into another kind of universe. A galaxy of huge spotlights hung suspended from the length and breadth of the high ceiling. Some dimming down from the previous scene, others still at full power awaiting the cue for the next set-up.

Then there was 'the man' – unexpectedly boyish looking, his back slightly turned away from us, surrounded by a group of the tech and camera crews, until he suddenly seemed to sense there was something going on around the back of him. He did a slow turn, travelled his eyes quickly across the four of us and then smiled.

'Well, the Air Crew has arrived – welcome to the war, fellas, good to see you.'

We didn't know whether to bend a knee or prepare to shake hands – Kubrick extended his and in turn we all shook it.

'Ben,' he called out, 'show the boys what they're getting into here.'

Kubrick half turned away, gesturing a 'see you later', and we trooped off after Ben. The place was bubbling with activity from electricians, gaffers, special effects and sound crews, prop men, scurrying wardrobe people, set dressers and decorators.

But dominating everything, all of it from its suspended height above the studio floor, was the silent, still and ominous hulk of the Bomber. Startlingly like the real thing except for a cut-away opening near the front section to allow the camera crew access to what was going on inside the flight deck. A construction team was turning the last nuts and bolts on the tower that would hold them close to it. We were cautioned, when the time came, to tread that side of the deck area with care. It would be some drop to the studio floor.

The first assistant walked up behind us, pointing up to the Bomber.

'Well, there it is, fellas, your home for the next 13 weeks.'

'Does it have central heating?' quipped Igor.

'Just pretend you're back in Russia,' muttered Frank through clenched teeth.

We shook a lot of hands that first day and did our damnedest to take in everything that was pointed out to us, but there was so much going on and so many people we just couldn't take it all in – even Igor stayed in neutral.

On the way out we were handed our call sheets for the next day's schedule with the times to report for make-up and wardrobe and the scenes to be shot. At the studio door I looked back a moment to see Kubrick getting into a huddle with Peter Sellers and Sterling Hayden. Before we reached the door handle, he'd glanced over and given us a nod and a slight wave – roll on tomorrow.

Next morning, on the dot of 7.00am, we reported for duty in our newly issued flight togs and began the first of many climbs up the ladder to the Bomber's side entry and into the war. The operations deck was no lounge room, hardly a spare centimetre of space anywhere – we were in for a cosy stay. Cosy and eerily isolated, high above the floor and everyone else, except for the camera crew perched at the side opening. We could have been in orbit around the moon for all we knew of what was going on at floor level. But there were exceptions and one was a classic!

Kubrick had set up a wild, no-holds-barred custard cream pie-throwing bash to be staged right across the War Room set, involving every major player in the film – every Minister, Chief of Staff and delegate from anywhere was a target.

The fight went on for almost three days and it took something like 200 fresh cream pie deliveries to keep it going. Everybody, including Peter Sellers, George C Scott, Keenan Wynn and Sterling Hayden, ended up a mess. The studio and everything in it was a mess; the only one to escape being smothered in dessert was Kubrick. The dry cleaning bill must have soared into the thousands, but all to no avail. The producers, not elaborating on their reasons, decided to eliminate the scene in total. Sorry you had to miss it.

A bizarre happening that came close to ending in tragedy was Sellers' fall from grace when pointing out a particular grievance to Kubrick. Unfortunately, Sellers, as the pilot, was standing at the opening to the flight deck at the time and the force of his argument carried him over the rim and into a drop of some considerable height onto the studio floor below. The resulting broken leg convinced Sellers that high altitudes were now out. He dropped the pilot's role and was soon back spinning his usual magic with the role of Dr Strangelove, but now strapped into a wheelchair to accommodate the recuperating limb fracture.

It was and remains one of cinema's most extraordinary performances.

Now, who to get to replace him? Kubrick hit the jackpot again. He remembered an old Hollywood hand named Slim Pickens, who'd made dozens of Westerns with one of the most distinctive twangs west of the Sierra Madre mountains. But recently he was spending most of his time at his ranch, training trick horses to perform in front of film cameras, and Stanley wasn't at all sure they'd get him. The production office wired Pickens' agent, who put the proposal to him along with an impressive list of inducements – a considerable pile of greenbacks, first class travel to England and working with Kubrick. Pickens apparently deliberated for about five seconds and he was in. He packed his bags, left his stables in the hands of a trusted foreman and arrived at Shepperton Studios to take over the pilot's seat and score the screen triumph of his career.

As for us, we happily crewed for some 13 more weeks on the film, trying to keep the blunders to a reasonable minimum. None of us could remember a moment when we wished we were doing anything else.

I'm convinced that Stanley wasn't concerned about how polished our rookie performances were. He wanted them enthusiastic yes, believable yes, but smoothly expert, I don't think so. We were young and untried, we bumped into things and dropped others and didn't always react in a cool, professional kind of way in tricky situations, but I think that's what he wanted. I hope so; it would have been at least payment in part for the simple truths he brought home to us. Mainly, how to grasp a character and, with just little things, be able to maintain it through the length of a film, no matter what was put in the way. 'It was,' he'd say, 'just a matter of give and take. That's what I try to do.'

He's left a few memories that still come back in play every so often.

We met again some 35 years later when his wife arranged a meeting at an exhibition near Oxford called 'Art in Action', in which she had a show of some of her paintings. He pulled up in a vintage Mercedes, slid out of the driver's seat and came over, hand outstretched, dressed as he most always was in an open checked shirt, work pants and shoes that still needed buffing. For a man reputed to have turned almost reclusive, he was warm and welcoming and just as naturally disarming as I'd always remembered him. A lot of our conversation eased back into the filming misadventures of *Dr Strangelove* and what still gave him a kick was the catalogue of misadventures by his freshman crew – which bits he'd dared leave in and which gaffes he felt were just too unbelievable. It was a warm July day, not a cloud in view, and our encounter was near sublime.

Chapter Two

I'd come to England first in the mid-1950s as lead singer in a vocal trio called The Three Deuces, a name spirited away from a legendary Jazz Nitery in New York. On my left and singing a rousingly expressive tenor line was Paul Summerville and holding down the bass clef was our Ukranian Canadian soul mate, Johnny Wacko.

We were all employed as disc jockeys and general programmers in a mid-sized suburban radio station with the call letters CKLB Oshawa, just outside Toronto. Oshawa, aside from being the General Motors capital of Canada, was also the birthplace of Authors and Swinson, a mind-bending magical mime act parodying the records of Mario Lanza, Spike Jones and Harry Lauder – and the only Canadian Variety act to break into the star-filled line-up at the London Palladium. They'd dropped back to Oshawa for a breather during a European tour and ended up taking over our lives.

At that time, Paul, Johnny and myself were engaged in some truly monumental affronts to the radio listening public as *The Shane and Fletcher Show*, which aired at 6.00am daily and, fortunately for Oshawa listeners and myself, was missed by just about everybody. I was supposedly in charge of the programme along with an unreal and wildly unmanageable budgerigar named Fletcher, who developed an outrageous talent for continually interrupting on mike, spilling coffee on the weather reports and interchanging the name of one sponsor's product for another's completely different one. The programme was as inane as the title suggests, but fantasies like these tend to take wing when you're trying to beat the boredom of spinning a turntable for most of the day.

It was at this point that Authors and Swinson happened by. Barry Authors, who could have retailed deep-freezers to Eskimos, somehow sold us on the idea of forming an American-style vocal act and taking off on a world tour with them. Howard Swinson, with a spiralling mop of hair that defied gravity, would nod sagely in agreement as if the whole thing would be a cinch.

Before we could collect our senses, we were sailing away from the dockside at Quebec City, bound for England on the *SS Homeric* and then rehearsing desperately for a ten-minute act of songs and patter for a gala last night concert as 'special guests'. Authors had negotiated this in exchange for our top cabin class accommodation and three invitations to the Captain's table on the way over. I spent a few nights by the ship's rail looking out over the never-ending expanse of sea, wondering if I should end it all now or wait until we were deported from England for fraud.

The sea had been as still as a pane of glass for practically the entire voyage and then came the last night Gala Celebration. Halfway through our programme in the concert room we were hit amidships by a sudden Force Six sea squall. The microphone sped away and skidded 30 feet across to the farthest side of the concert room floor just as Johnny, our poet in residence, hit a high point in his verse salute to a local Lady of the Night while we harmonised 'May the Good Lord Bless and Keep You' in the background. *Sunday Night at the London Palladium* it wasn't.

We were almost worse than terrible. But it got better.

In Britain at that time, although it wasn't to last a lot longer because of the explosive development of the television industry, the place to see and hear your favourite showbusiness entertainers was the local variety theatre. Every city and town had them. Performers would travel the country, appearing on the bill of a different theatre every week; they were masters of their craft and the audiences loved them.

There would be a 'headliner' and six or seven supporting acts, and that's where we started. We seldom if ever hung out in our dressing room but stood in the wings most every night to see how the top performers went about it – watched entranced as the best stand-up comics, high-wire acts, acrobats and mystifying illusionists transformed the bare boards of the stage into something magical, out of this world and near hypnotic.

We began to learn how to shape an act – marked how the top-liners handled the toughest kinds of audience and gradually got to them, how they'd use lighting and pace and mood, worked out over long years on stage. It could be a veritable lion's den or a sea of smiling faces and they walked out there 14 times a week, sometimes wondering, especially on matinées, if the pit pianist would show up – and sometimes wishing he hadn't!

We ended up playing every Number One date in the country with the exception of the London Palladium. Ironically, that was finally offered to us as we were on our way to a booking in New York at the Palace Theatre, the legendary mecca of American showbusiness. We opened the week following Judy Garland's triumphant return to Broadway. She drew thousands and turned New York over – we played to hundreds and were the best-kept secret in town.

But we'd cracked it, the three of us, The Three Deuces. We'd travelled 7000 miles and nabbed one of the most sought-after vaudeville dates in the whole of America. We were still walking on air ten days after we closed. But it's strange the way the unthinkable comes into play at times like these. After deliberating for some time, I chose another kind of walk shortly after that, for better or worse – to leave the act and go out on my own. The trio was pretty secure now, following the week at the Palace; offers were coming in from both the US and Canada. The act's future might not carry a gold-plated guarantee, but it was definitely a rosier one than before.

But Paul was a close friend, we'd been through two radio stations together, teamed up on play-by-play baseball and hockey broadcasts and spent some memorable times around the piano keeping a number of late-night cabaret clubs going till dawn's early glow. It wasn't easy to take a first step away from all that.

I had a long-held yearning to act and maybe this was the time. Rifts were starting to appear in the act, not between Paul and myself, but they were happening. After a late-night heart to heart we decided that if there was going to be a move it had better be now. We both knew, I think, that we'd stay in touch and meet up when we could, and most probably recall and probably elaborate on the good times and the not so good of that very vital part of both our lives ... Winter digs in West Hartlepool, where a heated stone would be placed in your bed to counteract the below-freezing temperature inside the house. Pacing the platform at Crewe Station on a Sunday afternoon between variety dates, when the place was so deserted you'd lay odds the plague was back in town. Then the pleasure of walking off stage at the finale of the act to a warm, enveloping kind of ovation you could never get enough of.

We had us some times, Paul.

★ ★ ★

So the move had been made, now what to do with it? I had lamentably little acting experience outside of playing in stage revues and radio dramas around Toronto and I needed some kind of – okay – *any* kind of acting mention to fill in the blank spaces in my log book. After three days of wandering around New York, looking up at theatre marquees lit with play titles and the actors cast in them, I ran into a producer acquaintance from London who was holding auditions for Noël Coward's coming production of *Nude With Violin*. He suggested I come along. It might be a good way to start breaking into the New York theatre scene.

'Well,' I said, 'you wouldn't want me playing the nude, but I'd be even worse at the violin' – which in terms of a self-help response must have come in around zero.

'You won't need to. Just come along and sing. You never know.'

I borrowed a friend's library card, got into the Noël Coward section, took out a song sheet entitled 'Matelot', which seemed to have a faint resonance to it, then hurried it back to my room to try to drum it, however sketchily, into my head.

I arrived the next day for the audition. There were two people in the audience, one of whom was Noël Coward. There was no mistaking that mandarin face and those piercing blue eyes. I took a brief run-through of the intro, set the tempo and then we were into it. For some unfathomable reason Coward's presence didn't inhibit me in the slightest. In fact it was quite the reverse. My voice suddenly opened, there was nothing in the way. I mis-cued on a line or two of the lyrics and just inserted my own, hardly an improvement. I don't think I looked at him after that. I finished up, took a slight bow and headed for the wings.

Two hands clapping in an empty auditorium can be a truly hollow sound. But that very much depends on where it's coming from. The applause from Noël Coward seemed to fill the theatre. Then I heard his voice, clipped but surprisingly warm.

'Mr Rimmer,' he said, 'don't go quite yet. I enjoyed the song and I certainly enjoyed your voice singing it. But I am afraid that your rather distinctive colonial tones wouldn't fit terribly easily into our salon style of presentation. But I do thank you for coming along. Maybe next time.'

It was the most encouraging turn-down I was ever likely to get. It doesn't come along that often. But then neither does a Noël Coward.

I walked off stage feeling as if my feet were treading on ozone. Now I felt ready to get on with it, wherever 'it' was going to lead me.

Two days later I booked a one-way Air Canada ticket from New York to my home town in Toronto and arrived an hour later. At first glance, except for a few untapped entrées into the Canadian Broadcasting and TV Corporation, my prospects seemed even slimmer than my wallet. First and most important was to acquire an 'agent' – and there I got very lucky.

There was an agency, established since I'd been away, located almost next door to the CBC and run by a 5'2" bundle of talent-promoting dynamite named Sylvia Train. TrainCo hadn't been around nearly as long as the more established offices, but already it was developing a reputation for singling out new and hi-potential talents and then placing them where they could be seen and best developed. And by now there was hardly a producer's or director's office that wouldn't pick up the phone and listen to what she had to say.

So we hooked up, she taking a bigger risk than I was. The drama roles were small, even minuscule at first, but gradually the parts grew into minor support roles and then into major ones and then into an unexpected breakthrough. I had to call on all those past singing years in theatres and clubs to have any kind of chance at it at all.

The CBC had decided to dig into its vaults to bankroll its most expensive and ambitious modern musical ever. It was to be called *Creator of Love* and would star probably the finest songstress that Canada had ever produced, Shirley Harmer. To co-star they needed a male counterpart, written as a rough-hewn, 'down home' guitar-strumming singer, with few of the known graces.

In most people's minds they already had the performer to play the role. His name was Robert Goulet and he had been a singing force on both sides of the border long before I'd put down a stake. Maybe it was because they were looking for a new face, I don't know, but after a bare rehearsal room audition with the director and a sound man (and what might have been the presence of a haunting, mandarin-faced onlooker) they offered me the role, though I still think Goulet was the better man for it. But he stamped his credentials just a year later, when he appeared as Sir Galahad to Richard Burton's King Arthur in one of the most memorable musicals of all time – Lerner and Loewe's *Camelot*. I never matched that one, Robert.

Creator of Love wasn't in the same league as *Camelot* but it scored a hefty success across Canada and Europe. It was a pleasant, middle-of-the road score and I was pretty comfortable with it. My chief difficulty was in trying to situate my fingers in a realistic playing position for the proper guitar chords and not have it look as though I was shearing sheep in the Aussie outback. Shirley Harmer held the fort, looked like an angel and sang like one, adding even more lustre to an already glittering chanteuse career.

For me, it was moving from the entrance level to landing on the first floor. Trainco, wasting little time, then arranged an appointment for me on that first floor with one of the most influential programme planners in the CBC. It was a crucial one.

Len Starmer was the head of light entertainment production at the CBC. I knew him only distantly, but I was about to get to know him a lot better. He was a gentleman, a man of his word, and unique in that he held one of the power point positions in the Corporation and had the wattage to use it well. His office room was 105. I trust I'll never forget it. I was ushered in at 11.30am and walked out at 12.15pm, clutching a contract offer for a 13-part weekly TV series as 'host and singer' – to be titled *Come Fly With Me*.

The idea was a 'musical road trip' to be filmed by a TV crew of four and myself, first across America with stop-over episodes in New York, Chicago, Los Angeles and New Orleans, then northward into Canada to Vancouver and Montreal, featuring a guest star in each city. The continental leg was almost too tasty to think about. Paris, Rome, London and then Brussels. I didn't know where I was going to end up next lifetime, but I thought maybe I'd put in for a re-run here.

Most of the time we were running to a grinding, split-minute schedule, gulping coffee and munching sandwiches in the back seats of taxis, just catching another plane or train and occasionally missing one. Ever spent the hours between 9.00pm and midnight in Des Moines Iowa Airport? It was eerie and practically empty. Only two people were in view, having a tête à tête at the far end of the terminal, and we could hear it word for word all the way across the departure area. The acoustics came crystal sharp, probably because there were so few people around to absorb the sound.

While the director and First Assistant got busy planning the next day's schedule, I looked round, spotted a local newspaper abandoned on an empty seat and picked it up in the hope of finding out what was happening in the world outside Des Moines. Nothing apparently! Maybe anything occurring beyond the Iowa State border, with the possible exception of an all-out nuclear dust-up, didn't rate even a mention. I dropped back in my seat, turned to the entertainment section and contented myself with catching up on the latest comic strip adventures of Lil' Abner and the Green Hornet.

The Des Moines sit-over was really the only dead time on the tour; otherwise it was chock full of glorious sights, never-before-heard sounds and walk-in characters who never stopped delighting. The street-marching Dixie jazz bands, the shoreline sweep of Lake Michigan under the multiplex skyline of Chicago, and finally, after a descending flight path over the length of Manhattan, the touchdown at Idlewild Airport. It was dazzling and overwhelming – what could top it?

Maybe one thing. An end of the American tour dinner at probably the most celebrity-frequented restaurant in New York – Toots Shoors. Unless you were a world heavyweight boxing champion, a 6'8" basketball centre forward for the home town Knickerbockers or the city's reigning District Attorney, you'd be lining up all night. Bob Goulet had dropped in a couple of nights previously and had graciously left his marker. The doorman, outfitted in a shade of Irish green that would have paled a piece of Tipperary turf, nodded us an entry and, seconds later, the crew and I sank gratefully into our waiting seats and ordered a premium bottle of vintage Burgundy.

Halfway through the second course, we had a totally unexpected visit to the table from the legendary host of the establishment, Toots Shoor, looking startlingly like a first cousin to the actor Victor McLaglen from *The Quiet Man*. After about ten minutes of salty conversation, he looked across the room to the Maître d', who was signalling him over to other patrons at another table.

'Back to business I'm afraid – hang around a little longer, will you?'

He got to his feet, nodded to all of us and headed back across the room, throwing a goodbye wave over his shoulder. Less than five minutes later, a waiter arrived hugging another bottle of the vintage Burgundy.

'You the folks from over the border? Compliments of Mr Shoor.'

With that he flourished the bottle, rested it gently on the table and left the rest to us.

So, a wonderfully enjoyable end to the first leg of our North American cavalcade. We called over a goodnight and thank you to our host, exited the restaurant in a totally disorderly fashion, tipped the doorman, who, catching a glimpse of the total, summoned a taxi with a whistle that would have wakened the sleeping citizens back in Yonkers, and we were off into the night.

Could we keep it going? The odds looked pretty good.

Our first European touchdown was at Rome Airport – Leonardo Da Vinci had been dead for centuries, but nobody had yet thought of naming an airport after him. The fact that he'd drawn up plans for the first flying machine over 500 years before didn't seem to have connected with anybody, even though some of the aircraft parked on the tarmac looked as though they might have slipped off his design table.

We managed a few afternoon set-ups with your host walking by the Colosseum, the Forum and the Trevi Fountain. In the evening we brought things further up to date. The Via Veneto was like a living, breathing set out of the film *La Dolce Vita* with its cafés, restaurants, haute couture boutiques and brightly marquee'd clubs. It was the main artery for Rome's newest 'celeb generation' and they packed the area all three nights we were there – some tucked away at end tables, others quite openly, unconcerned with all the staring.

Hollywood players taking an evening's breather from their filming in and around Rome, Kirk Douglas, Jack Palance, Shirley MacLaine and Rod Steiger, would be holding down tables at the outdoor cafés – along with the likes of Anita Ekberg, Elsa Martinelli, Marcello Mastroianni and Federico Fellini.

On our second night, from a nearby table I inadvertently traded a glance with Fellini – I felt I was suddenly being measured for a close-up. Meantime the sidewalk parade continued, some passers-by tripping over themselves to catch a celebrity and cars doing about the same up and down the Via Veneto's streaming traffic lanes. The area was rife with non-stop horn-hooting and some pretty imaginative hand gestures with expletives never deleted.

There were more and different visual delights at our next stop, Venice.

Here's a verse from a song that appeared in the New York revue *New Faces of 56*, in which Eartha Kitt made her Broadway debut.

> *Waltzing in Venice with you*
> *Isn't so easy to do.*
> *If you should take one more step than you oughta*
> *You vill be doing the valtz under vater.*

Well, I've always liked it.

So, if you can keep from going under and instead skim over the canals in one of hundreds of Venetian gondolas or water taxis, the rewards are magical – lantern-lit bridges, cobble-stoned lanes, passages, open squares, majestic Duomos and rows of lofty, multi-painted villas rising steeply out of the waters of over 170 canals. Then Piazza San Marco, the city's splendid, spacious and historical gathering place, dominated by the high-domed Basilica Cathedral with its rooftop viewing walkways and four copper sculpted horses charging high over the entrance. It's a sight that everyone should allow themselves once in a while.

Our stay lasted only two days and in all too brief a time we put the clapboard on our final sunset shots of the bay, crawled back to our hotel rooms for a light kip, and started the next morning with a couple of dynamite Expressos that had us jumped up and ready for anything. After an 18-kilometre drive to the airport, we boarded an Air France flight, finished our on-board breakfast with servings of flaked Parisienne pastry, and were motoring up the Champs Elysées by mid afternoon.

Tough life eh, Asterix?

The Avenue takes you past some of the most stunning terraced facades of any major city on the continent. Conversely, the average Parisian has the unenviable reputation of being one of the most cynical, hard-nosed urban dwellers in all of Europe. *Allons*, let's find out! Most of our little Canuck troupe had gone through varying levels of conversing in what was called 'Quebec patois' – an earthy mix of French, Iroquois and Eskimo tongues familiar to most inhabitants of eastern and maritime Canada. We decided to sound it out to see if it would breach the wall of French indifference we seemed to be colliding with everywhere.

First stop was at a café and bar next door to the hotel. Over our first glasses of wine, and with as many shrugs and gestures as we could think of, we entered into a conversation about the day's adventures. That was about as far as it got. There was suddenly a hush you could have cut with a cleaver. Our eyes travelled around the room to find everyone staring across at us as if we'd collectively broken wind at our end of the bar. The bartender rolled his eyes and gingerly backed up to his dispenser. We finished our drinks, shrugged an apology to the café habitués, then sidled out watching each other's backs, figuring that while we were still able to, we'd head back to the safety of the hotel.

On our next and last day, we turned back to our guidebook French, stuck our noses and cameras into the foyers and back tables of a succession of famed Latin Quarter night spots like the Crazy

Horse, Pigalle and Apache, then took a short walk to stand quietly in the Place Saint Michel, just an intersection away, to marvel at the splendour of its sculpted fountain flanked closely by a guardian dragon on either side. That night we confirmed our flight arrangements to Brussels, maybe wondering who'd be the next one to put their foot in it, managed a scant four hours' sleep and next morning, while the street cleaners were out making Paris look proper again, made our way to the airport, passing the glorious spread of the Gardens of Versailles on the way. Things looked back on track.

Well almost, except for one memorable moment in Brussels, when our esteemed but sometimes accident-prone director, trying to adjust the film gear on the cameraman's shoulder from behind, toppled both of them into the sheer glass entrance door to Sabena Airlines, shattering it completely.

As a platoon of staff and officials swept in to scoop up the fractured array of glass lying everywhere across the airport floor, we signalled our porters to follow us on the double and scrambled down the passageway toward the boarding area and a safe passage to London and then back to Canada, hoping there wouldn't be a restraining order from Interpol awaiting our return. Happily the only reception committee present was a small corps of newsmen firing questions about our jaunt across Europe and America. Much relieved, we settled comfortably into our interviews and ceased looking back over our shoulders.

The next week, back at the CBC, studio preparations for *Come Fly With Me* began in earnest, with song, dance and orchestral run-throughs and the final editing of the travel footage, most of which had already been expressed back from each of the filming locations. In a breathtakingly short time we were into our 12-week summer series. The rehearsal pace had been so frenetic it had given us little time to worry too much about how it would go over – luckily, it did. The ratings well justified the time and the outlay, including the cost of one reinforced replacement door for the Sabena Airlines offices in Brussels.

The choreographer on the show was a delectable and talented young lady named Deirdre Lester, who, we were to discover later, was married to the London-based American film and TV director Richard Lester. He had flown over to catch the last show of the series, which happily had Barry Morse appearing as our guest star. He sang the most touching rendition of 'I've Grown Accustomed To Her Face' – nobody could have done it better.

Dick Lester – who was about to return to England to direct *The Running Jumping & Standing Still Film* – was so swept away by the show he offered me a booking on a British TV spectacular with Ella Fitzgerald in two months' time. Did I say YESSSSSSSSS!!!?

Chapter Three

My contract date with Dick Lester in England allowed just enough time to take up a feature film offer. I suppose I scored some sort of distinction in being seen as the only blue-eyed North American Indian east of the Rockies. The vast majority entered the world either brown or grey-eyed. But fame can arrive in strange ways.

My role would be that of Little Chief Running Bear, leading brave and first son of the present Chief Standing Bear. The film bore the title *Flaming Frontier*, with a young and lusty lead called Jim Davis, who 20 years later would be doing the same sort of role in the TV series *Dallas*. The Kleinberg Studios on the outskirts of Toronto were chosen as the launch pad for this production. The studios had been erected on the grounds of a working ranch, occupied by two large corrals, a clapboard bunkhouse for the hired hands and stables for a dozen horses, one of which was my own, a dappled grey, two-year-old half-Arabian filly named Aziel.

My first few scenes in the story were hardly demanding, but the big one, leading a band of bloodthirsty young braves into a sidelong attack on a passing wagon train, would take something extra. I wasn't too bad a horseman then, but being the leader of a gang of screaming braves going at a full gallop, knee-hugging a small 'Indian blanket' in place of a saddle, was breathtakingly daunting.

The scene called for our pack to come charging over the brow of a hill, then wheel abruptly to the right in pursuit of the wagon train. The camera crew would be in place half way down the other side to catch the swerve of the chase, with myself leading the charge. So up the hill we charged and in less than a minute my blanket was sliding back around the horse's haunches. I reached out and managed to get a hold of Aziel's mane in an attempt to stay aboard – unfortunately all that did was increase the tempo of his gallop. I felt I was riding on top of a cement mixer.

As we came down over the brow of the hill, Aziel swept to the right as planned, then skidded into a half cartwheel but somehow managed to scramble back on all fours. I, meantime, had left the horse and the blanket and gone into free flight straight towards the camera crew, who just stood there, totally immobilised by what was happening.

I landed smack in the middle of them, the loader, focus puller, grip, operator, everyone except the cameraman, who managed to launch himself out of the way in the nick of time. After we'd regained our feet, dusted ourselves off and checked for fractures, the director called a rethink. It was decided that, on the next take, they would fit the horse with a flat saddle, cover it with a heavy blanket, and rope me to it in a slumped position so I would appear as the first casualty of the raid. They would also stick me in the middle of the pack so, if anything untoward happened, it would be covered by the rest of the attacking Indians.

I almost turned in my headband. But I wasn't their only problem.

The film was being shot in the newly developed Panavision system, which considerably enlarged the focal breadth of what was being filmed. It was something that the Canadian film world had little experience with. The next day's rushes looked absolutely ravishing, as did the motor scooters leaning up against trees, jet tracks all over the sky and gigantic silos on the horizon, all of which nobody had invented yet. I mean, this was meant to be back in the mid-1700s.

An immediate re-shooting schedule was drawn up and camera adjustments worked out to discourage any of the producers from taking out their investment backing and decamping. That left my attack party of Indian braves, still under layers of war paint, sitting on the hillside wondering how best to pass the time until the shoot geared up again. Then around the bend we observed the approach of an aged Model T Ford stacked to the roof with cartons of eggs, making its way lazily towards the film caterer's caravan further down the road.

It was like some instant kind of symbiosis that struck all of us at the same time. All eyes switched themselves to their Little Chief Running Bear – me. I gave back a stiff-jawed Jeff Chandler nod, raised my hand and with a blood-curdling 'Whoop!' led the braves pell mell down the hill towards the egg delivery van – all of us armed to the teeth with lances, bows, arrows and tomahawks.

At that point, the egg man looked up and spotted us. The car lurched to a violent stop, and then tipped slightly into a nearby ditch. Egg boxes flew in every direction and the narrow road was covered by the largest spread of scrambled eggs you were ever likely to see in your life. The egg man emerged from the Model T, eyes frozen in shock at the line of fully armed Indian braves a few feet in front of him, and immediately raised his hands – then on a closer look he put them down again.

'You fellas all havin' a bit of fun, huh?'

There was no fear in his eyes now. He pointed to the road, still swimming in 25 yards of broken eggs.

'That's quite a bit of spoilage on the road there.'

It was just about time to call a halt to our war games. I took a step towards him.

'Look, we're sorry, we were just bored to death. We'll reimburse you for everything and we'll clear it all up, okay. You sure you're all right?'

There was enough of a nod back to reassure us he was.

We all chipped in to raise the 50 dollars, added another 20 and handed it over to him. This time we got a smile with the nod. I motioned the braves to the front of the car. We shouldered the bumper and eased the car, still intact, back onto the road.

Next day, when we were getting ready to re-shoot the Indian attack scene, the Ford rounded the bend again, then paused. The egg man peered out the driver's window to check for another ambush ahead. We all got to our feet and waved him on. He eased back and rattled past, just a little faster than the day before. Further on we saw his hand hang out his window to give back a half wave.

'Looks like eggs are back on the menu,' one of the braves said.

★ ★ ★

Now back to the deal that TrainCo had negotiated with Dick Lester for the TV spectacular. Just to top it up, Sylvia Train talked the Austin-Healey Car Company in Toronto into arranging a courtesy Sprite sports car to be made available on my arrival in London. So once more to the airport and another goodbye to my mother, father and sister Noreen, who must have been wondering if I was ever going to stay in one place long enough to send on a postcard.

The British ABC Television channel had secured the rights to produce the spectacular in just two weeks' time. But with just one week to go they were also the bearer of some crushing news. Ella Fitzgerald, due to a recurrence of an illness that had plagued most of her singing career, had been forced to cancel all her UK and European bookings, including the spectacular. Ouch!

So there I was in London, motoring around in a 'racing green' sports car with hardly enough money to fill the petrol tank half way and not one sane reason for hanging on. Then somebody rubbed a magic lamp, Dick Lester added a little arm-twisting, and ABC TV, who were preparing to produce a series of *Armchair Theatre* plays by American TV writers, signed me up for two of them. The first thing I did was fill up the petrol tank, then I opened the scripts.

Tad Mosell and Ed James were two of television's leading writers out of New York – Mosell would later go on to win the 1961 Pulitzer

Prize for Drama for his stage play *All the Way Home*. Both productions were aired by ABC in the UK and both rang up some very respectable viewing figures. ABC was hoping to extend these New York based dramas into a TV series, but at the time its confirmed market outlets were just not strong or numerous enough. The sales revenues did eventually produce the kind of figures they'd been hoping for, but by then it was too late. The money men wanted quicker returns and had moved elsewhere. But I decided to hang in there, busying my phone with as many job enquiries as I could think of, short of one bleak notice offering a steeplejack apprenticeship.

Suddenly 'bleak' became 'break' when a call came through from Dick Lester with an invitation to join him at ABC TV, where he was putting together a late-night show of comedy sketches and music to be titled *After Hours*. The show would be beamed solely into the Midlands, detouring London, which seemed a mysterious omission. Ex-Goon Michael Bentine would headline proceedings in close cahoots with Dick Emery, Clive Dunn (later Corporal Jones in *Dad's Army*), Benny Lee and the Johnny Dankworth Orchestra. Cleo Laine and myself were the singers and occasional bit players and, ah, that girl could sing. To many people's ears and certainly mine, the warmest sound since Ella.

It was the kind of show that Dick Lester had produced successfully in Philadelphia and should have been allowed to play to a larger audience here. It was brilliant stuff, even the out-takes were special. Who knows what's at work in the minds of programme planners.

So, a little dispirited, I made my way homeward to north London. I dropped my bag and unlocked the front door – to the insistent ringing of the telephone from my flat, four flights up. I didn't quite manage to break my leg in getting to it. To my surprised delight the call was from an old friend, Norman Newell, Artist & Repertoire head of Columbia Records, who had recorded the Three Deuces to a couple of respectable hit parade contenders. One, 'Sh Boom Sh Boom', I can still hear ringing in my head.

'Norman, it's great to hear from you.'

'Your singing is sounding rather good these days.'

'Nice to hear, how do you know?'

'We recorded two *After Hours* programmes monitoring Cleo Laine and there you were. You sounded fine. Would a bit more singing interest you?'

'The last ones didn't go that well, did they?'

The previous recording session with Norman Newell and musical director Geoff Love had been on two sides of a 45 rpm disc – an English version of the French chanson 'The Three Bells' and the Fats Domino R&B chart number 'I Want To Walk You Home'. The disc really didn't get out of the starting gate. They were either the wrong songs or the wrong singer.

'Sorry, we just couldn't get it moving. But I've got one that's a winner!'

'What is it – a Hitler speech set in E flat?'

'I'm not going to tell you any more about it – but I know you'll love it.'

Well, he sent it and I liked it, and in nine days' time I passed through EMI's Abbey Road Studios clutching a well-rehearsed vocal score of 'Wagon Train' – the signature song of the TV series, sung, and rousingly, by Frankie Laine. Somebody high up among the musical corridors of Columbia Records had decided that another version could work well for European and Far East distribution. I got around the piano in Studio C with Norman in charge of the session and Geoff Love's orchestra and we knocked it off in an afternoon.

I don't think our version dented Frankie Laine's European sales, but in Japan and Hong Kong ours rose to number two in the charts and for the next year I was hopping back and forth to the bank, exchanging yen for sterling, hoping that it was all legal and there wouldn't be a Ninja hit man lurking in some darkened doorway ready to reach out and detach me from my latest royalty cheque.

Before long, I was going through the same Abbey Road doors once more, this time with a new label, MFP – Music for Pleasure – and three new partners in song, the eternally sparkling Lionel Blair and Stella Tanner and the former singer with the Ted Heath Band, Dennis Lotis. We just had enough time to brush cheeks before we were squired down the stairs to recording studio B. The place was even more spacious than I remembered it, vast enough to house a full symphony orchestra and probably half the Albert Hall as well. The walls were hung almost ceiling to floor with huge baffle boards to subdue any extraneous sound. It had all the ambience of an abandoned London Underground Station and took a little time getting used to. But the studio welcome from Norman and Geoff nicely cut through all that.

The MFP label was being introduced to cover the mid-ground market between traditional and pop. Plans were already afoot for a full repertoire of light classics and Broadway and film musicals.

Lionel and Stella behaved with surprising ease, nobody crashed into a microphone or wandered into another's song lines and *On the Town* was a take. So enthused were Columbia over the European-wide reception, they commissioned us to do three more musicals over the next year – *Seven Brides for Seven Brothers*, *Funny Girl* and *High Society*. The MFP label gave us a great kick to record, and we hoped the pleasure would reach out well beyond Abbey Road.

I'd hardly had time to turn around when a call came through from a booking agent in Frankfurt, with an offer of a USO Entertainment Tour for the American Forces in Germany, Turkey and a NATO base on the Bay of Naples. My horizon was lifting.

'I didn't know that the Americans were in Turkey,' I said.

'They run four Air Force bases, mainly reconnaissance as well as a place called Site 23.'

'That sounds a little sinister.'

'Don't be silly, it's an official American Government installation.'

Before I could think of anything suitable to reply to that, the

41

booker continued.

'It's some package you're on – a terrific dance duo, a new American comic and an Aussie singing accordionist act. Anyway, you've been out there before, haven't you?'

'Yes, with The Three Deuces, but we didn't go anywhere near Turkey.'

'Don't worry – it'll be a piece of cake.'

'Sure…'

The Deuces had been based in one of the most beautiful cities in the now Allied zone of Germany, Wiesbaden, during a previous USO Tour. It was just a short distance from Frankfurt on the Rhine, and during the smash and grab years of the Third Reich's trampling of Europe, Hitler was often taken there to bathe and drink the waters of this famous health spa retreat. Couldn't somebody have slipped in a poison pellet or maybe drained the pool?

When the American forces had taken over the area at the end of the carnage of World War II, they commenced a wholesale conversion programme of all standing installations to make room for housing the American military and their multi facilities. The second priority was the setting up of the kind of entertainment circuit that would keep up the morale of the American peace-keeping forces, most of them hardly out of their teens and away from home for the first time.

Almost immediately, with supplies flown in from depots right across America, night clubs began sprouting in threes at every US installation in the Zone, one for enlisted men, another for NCOs and the third, the Officers' Clubs; all were designed for what the 'forces' wanted most – hard tables, soft chairs and stacks of beer and entertainment.

Artist's agents were quick to find their way into this new showbusiness territory, bringing with them files, photos and the names of some of the top theatre, TV and club entertainers in Europe and America. Most of the old theatrical circuits had been bombed out and abandoned during the course of the war, but now, from everywhere, artistes flooded in – comics, conjurers, high-wire acts, acrobats, illusionists, dancers and singers, heading for these new and buzzing centres of entertainment. The clubs' bankrolls were almost limitless, funded in the main by rows of gleaming slot machines that rarely stood idle. They could afford anybody they wanted and they all came – Louis Armstrong, Bob Hope, Tony Bennett, Sarah Vaughan, Louis Prima, Billy Daniels and Red Skelton. It became a mirror image of Las Vegas.

The USAAF Headquarters based in Wiesbaden backed the new club circuit to the hilt – the floodgates were open, the clubs were jammed every night. So our touring troupe formed up – the Two Martinis dance act (formerly Three), headed by an alluring young lady named Sheila Logan; an exhilarating American comic, 'Chuckles' Walker; an Aussie accordionist called Molly D, and myself as host and singer.

Each troupe had now to present themselves at a gathering of Club Sergeants, who would then book the shows that they favoured for their particular clubs around the Zone – at times it came painfully close to lining up in a cattle auction. But at that opening audition and the next, we managed to nab the 'blue ribbon', which signified that we had been the choice of most of the bookers.

The tour was rolling, picking up 'appearance' requests in all the major club dates from Munich to Mainz, from Heidelberg to Rhine-Maine and then on to the most coveted booking of all, the crème de la crème of the USO Circuit, the NATO Officers Club spread high along the hills overlooking the Bay of Naples. The Isle of Capri glistened like a green jewel in the gentle seas of the Mediterranean the first time we saw it – little wonder Gracie Fields was so spellbound by it. The setting seemed to affect everyone in a similar way, including Sheila and me. We left the stage to a boisterous ovation.

Next morning our bleary-eyed troupe geared up and headed towards Turkey and the Aegean seaport city of Izmir. At first sight it was picture-postcard perfect, giving no inkling of the nightmare events that were to follow. Take a look at your next purchase of dates; chances are they were picked, attractively packaged and shipped from Izmir. The city was a teeming kaleidoscope of colour, vibrantly high-pitched sounds and a street energy that hadn't changed since the time of the Ottomans. We would stay the night here and then next morning would embark on our tour of American-manned Air Force bases at Ankara and Adana. There was a third stop at the tersely named map reference of Site 23 – it was, as we were to find out later, not just an 'installation', but a fully stocked rocket-launching base with every kind of ballistic missile locked on to targets in both Moscow and Leningrad. Nice sort of comfort site they'd landed us in, smack in the middle of a possible nuclear battle zone.

We were, however, blissfully unaware of all this, concerned above all with surviving our first experience in a Turkish touring coach, travelling on roads that would have daunted a mountain goat. Within the first half hour we had veered through four breakneck S bends, rumbled down and then up a half-dozen major pot holes, and at one point ground to a halt just in time to avoid an uprooted tree that had a girth of some 15 feet. By now we were hanging on for dear life, hoping the bus would splinter a tyre somewhere, anywhere, forcing a pit stop that would give us some relief and maybe the chance of a brief measure of sleep.

No such luck! Our man at the wheel, a reborn Ben-Hur, was determined to get through. In order to hold on and not slide off his seat during the longer hops, he would put on a series of loud, long-playing Dervish folk-dance tapes. These kept him at least partly conscious, but made the rest of us feel as if we were under attack by helicopters, hill tribesmen and herds of dinosaurs. Travelling is such fun!

Our appearances at Ankara and Adana were granted well over-the-top receptions. Though welcome, especially after our survival trials with one of the country's elite bus services, it made us feel slightly uneasy. When not responding exuberantly to the stage shows or maybe a half-dozen Budweisers and the down-home country music which blared without let-up in between, some of the troops appeared listless and somewhat hollow-eyed, as if locked into a waiting situation none of them was enjoying very much. They gave the impression of having been in that same place, going through the same motions for longer than they should have.

The following night we pulled into Site 23, which could have been anywhere in the Western Hemisphere, or the Eastern one for that matter, and performed the show to gung-ho applause. This was customary by now, but still a most welcome entrée to our final stop in Turkey. We hit the sack that night, grateful that we were now on the last lap of the tour and would soon be returning home.

The next morning – 21 October 1962 – a Red Alert came through from Washington, reporting that U-2 aerial photographs had confirmed the presence of medium and intercontinental range ballistic missile sites on Cuba, just off the coast of Florida. The rockets could reach all of the United States except for the Upper Western coast and all of Mexico and Central America as well. There was also the small matter of 40,000 Russian troops and 270,000 armed Cubans at the ready. President John F Kennedy ordered an immediate blockade of the island to prevent any further Russian arms shipments from being delivered. If Khrushchev chose to challenge the embargo, Kennedy vowed it would mean WAR!

Immediately, Site 23 and American bases everywhere went into full 'Nuclear Alert' – all incomings and outgoings were blocked at the gates. Inside Site 23 we became virtual prisoners of the very people we had come to entertain. No communication with the outside was possible, bar privileges inside were zeroed, and the tension, mounting rapidly in every quarter, was now so palpable you could smell it.

For six days the world held its breath and waited. Then on the 27th, Khrushchev edged back from the precipice at the eleventh hour by pledging to dismantle all missile sites on Cuba for good, and Kennedy followed through with a promise to call off any invasion plans for the island. Done!

They got the club bars back and running in record time, lifting the spirits and easing everybody's jitters. Joy spread everywhere. Officers embraced Sergeants, non-coms other non-coms, and enlisted men anybody they could grab. We came back on stage in the huge Site 23 NCO club, gave a celebratory concert for all the base personnel and got out of there the next morning, after hiding the driver's cherished collection of tapes.

Some hours later, we returned to the coastal town of Izmir, threading our way through ranks of painted carts, top-heavy with freshly caught squid, cucumbers by the kilo and piles of dates. Trading was carrying on as if nothing unusual had been happening over the past six days. Well, when in Izmir… We gathered up bags of fresh produce and left half an hour later for a spellbinding sail across the Aegean to the Italian sea port of Brindisi and, from there, overland through Greece and a memorable stay in the always stunning, white-walled city of Athens. Whether by accident or design, Sheila and I seemed to be side by side, more and more. Nice way to travel! Two days later, a high-speed transcontinental sped us up and through the Alps towards the Rhine area of Germany and our base at Frankfurt/Wiesbaden.

We'd had just enough time to drop our bags at the hotel reception when two messages were handed to us. The Martinis were reminded that they had two final cabaret dates to fill in Munich, and then Sheila had a meeting with an American booker in Wiesbaden to set up a UK-Euro Talent Agency that would handle international acts and clubs in both England and the American Forces Zone. My tour mate to be an 'impresario' – well, did you ever?

The call for me was from my agent, getting me back to London and into that life-boosting run of the Kubrick film. Which is pretty much where we came in.

Chapter Four

Following *Dr Strangelove*, the BBC was trolling around the North American acting community in London for someone to take the role of a hard-nosed, Yankee-type magazine editor. They'd have to cover a lot of ground. Unlike our Australian mates who were bunched mainly in the London sprawl of Earls Court, the American and Canadian contingents were more inclined to meld into any part of London that attracted them, as long as it was somewhere near a tube or rail line, a few inviting pubs and a late-night bus route.

A fine Toronto-born actor, Garrick Hagon (namesake of one of the 18th century's most illustrious actor-managers, David Garrick) found an impressive residence alongside the open spaces of Clapham Common; for him, it's now home. Angus MacInnes, who would turn up as a feature player in *Star Wars*, developed a yen for Scotland's north-east coast and settled down a caber toss or so from Edinburgh. He commutes from there to studios around London and the continent. Others found living space in the West Country, on board a house-boat on the Thames, and the rest around central London.

At the oddest times of day, you would hear American baseball scores and the latest in Australian-rules rugby piping out from platoons of transistors, criss-crossing anywhere from Camden Town to Kensington High Street to Covent Garden to more obscure points in between.

Meanwhile, the North American colony and anybody else who could come up with a mid-Atlantic or even a Mexican border accent was called into the BBC Television Centre for a listen to and a look over. It's still part of the system and it's still frightening. Surprisingly, the selection committee, possibly suffering hangovers from a previous night's knees-up at the BBC bar, marked their ballot in my favour. The consequences of that, even though they took some time to surface, shaped a number of unexpected events that would follow.

Compact was the serialised TV story of a weekly magazine, maybe a prototype of an early *Hello* or *OK*, reporting in graphic detail the antics, entanglements and excesses of the hi-flying celeb class. My name as newly appointed editor was Corrigan and the brief was to hoist *Compact's* viewing figures back up to the level they'd enjoyed a season or two previously – before *Coronation Street* began amassing the kind of viewing figures that had sponsors lining up to grab a piece of the cake.

My stay on the series went to its contracted six months, but the memories of that association have lasted a deal longer. You found yourself spending as much off-scene time watching and learning from the rest of the cast as you did memorising your lines. They were real, all of them, good-humoured, solid and easygoing, even when they were inevitably involved knee-deep in some personal dramas of their own. They never stinted, never offered less than was due to their fellow players – it was always 'the Full Monty'. And with the resurgence of *Coronation Street's* popularity, the pressure was always there not to let the gap in the ratings between the two major soaps widen. The most difficult part of it, especially when you've been in the same role for many months and many episodes, was to keep it fully fresh and alive and not to revert to mannerism.

The harder you work at it, the easier it looks and that for the viewer makes it comfortable watching. There were some past masters on that series – Robert Flemyng, Johnny Wade, Michael Caine's first wife Patricia Haines, and Bill Kerr. Their ensemble playing was just as Kubrick said it should be – 'give and take'.

Compact made it a contest for the next two seasons, but the magic mix of the script writing, the star status attained by many of the performers, and the high-spin publicity push by ITV got the *Street* out in front to stay. The BBC threw in the towel and brought *Compact* to a close in 1964.

★ ★ ★

Now, on a sunny summer's day in 1963, I was perched on a bench on the Chelsea side of the Thames, tapping one foot against the other and wondering where they were going to lead me next. But it's at times like this, if you're lucky, that a voice mysteriously like your own tells you to step away from all this tired kind of fretting, let the gaze go out – have yourself a look around, shake things up a bit.

On the way back to the flat I dialled a couple of other resting North American actors and met up with them at a favourite morning nook near Trafalgar Square called Lyons Corner House. It was one of the few places in London where they actually served coffee that didn't back up on you and get you twice in one gulp. The get-together lifted our collective angst, as happened in most meetings with other actors, and after pledging we'd be on the phone to each other the minute we heard of a casting anywhere, we split the bill, followed each other out the door and went our separate ways.

I heard the phone ringing as I reached the fourth flight of stairs to the flat in Chalcot Square and grabbed it on the final ring. It was Sheila, my boon travelling companion on our journey of discovery through Turkey, Greece and the high ground of the Alps. She had now started her UK Continental Booking Agency and opened an office in Piccadilly Circus.

'Hey, Sheila,' I gasped.

'You called me?'

'Yep, I did. I've decided it's high time I went to see your folks.'

That brought the slightest of pauses from the other end of the phone.

'Are you sure?'

'I'm tired of all the cloak and dagger stuff. We love each other, we want to get married. They should know about it.'

'I agree. When?'

'I think this weekend.'

'Do you want me to go with you?'

'Maybe as far as the front gate. I'll storm the ramparts myself. Okay?'

'You're my hero!'

'See you for dinner.'

Sheila's parents lived in a splendidly sprawling house in the middle of Tiptree village in Essex. Her father, John Pullar Logan, was the highly regarded Scottish local doctor, affectionately known as 'Doc'. He was admired around the county not only for the wealth of his medical know-how, but for the considered way he administered it. Sheila's mother Bess was the head of just about everything from the Women's Institute to the St John's Ambulance Brigade and was a leading light in the Essex Operatic Society.

As we approached the village after turning off the A12 highway, the gentle aroma rising from the spread of surrounding strawberry fields was suddenly everywhere. This was the home territory of Wilkins Tiptree jams, identified by a black and white labelled bottle that after 80 years still stocks the shelves of more grocers around the world than probably any other.

I had been cautioned by Sheila's brothers, John and David, that Bess, the matriarch of the family, might not be wild about the idea of her daughter being swept away by a coarse colonial adventurer, never to be seen again in the known world. They advised sticking a white handkerchief in my pocket to be taken out and waved at the first sign of trouble. They would await the outcome of my foray in the saloon bar of the Maypole pub just down the road. I felt like I was in the trenches and about to go over the top. I stood outside the entrance to the Logan home, pulled in a deep breath, passed through the wide wooden gates, past a multi-toned rose garden and a tennis court, undecided as to whether to walk tall or make myself as low a target as possible – half expecting a Gatling gun to open up from under the front windows. But 20 paces more and I was still standing; not a shot had been fired. I reached up and rapped twice on the solid brass knocker.

There was a slight thud as if a carpet was being shifted up against it from the inside, then a muffled 'Damn.' The door was opened by a very pleasant-looking middle-aged gentleman wearing a deep-pocket checked sports coat and carrying a pipe in the cup of his right hand.

'Dr Logan?' I asked.

He nodded and I added quickly, 'Sheila and I thought it would be a good idea if I dropped over and said hello. My name's Shane.'

'Ah yes, good, come in.'

He turned, beckoning me to follow, smoothing out a few rises in the carpet as he moved towards a half-open hall door revealing the side panel of a tall, mahogany cabinet inside. Bess was sitting in a large, brocaded easy chair dressed in a long, flowery frock and white summer shoes. Quite a formidable-looking lady and maybe not quite as welcoming as Doc had been. A few bumps on the road ahead looked more than likely.

But what kept the betrothal on course was partly Doc's faith in his daughter's judgment and partly the fact that my father, Thomas Deacon, boarded a Trans-Atlantic flight for the first time in his life, coming all the way from Toronto to help bolster the prospects of a Tiptree wedding. I consoled myself with Shakespeare's dictum that 'the course of true love never runs smooth'.

Sheila and I met my father at Heathrow Airport. He was sporting his navy blue blazer and grey flannels, and as it turned out we didn't have a thing to worry about. He and Doc formed an immediate alliance and Bess, similarly impressed, let go any misgivings. And so the marriage bans were prepared.

★ ★ ★

Thomas Deacon was quite a man. He was born in the Antrim Road area of Belfast in 1899 but was never tempted to become politically involved in the 'Troubles' that were spreading all around him. In fact, so fed up was he with the often mindless warmongering in that restless part of the city that as soon as his 16th birthday arrived – and looking older than his years – he reported to and was accepted by the British Army. He was quickly co-opted into the Communications Corps in France and found himself as a courier, biking top-level messages from one command post to another along the front line of the British trenches.

After the Armistice in 1918, he returned to Belfast and, with a brash bit of Irish blarney, got himself a job as a starting reporter on the *Belfast News Letter*. I guess he was pretty good because he became a permanent fixture of the paper – permanent but still penniless. Maybe it was the extra pint of Guinness one night that did it, but he soon dropped his job at the *News Letter* and finagled a steerage passage aboard an ocean liner bound for Boston USA – an arrangement for those with empty pockets and strong backs, able to shovel enough coal into the boiler room furnaces to get them to their destination. He would say later that he couldn't recall much of the ocean on the way over as he was stationed under the water line for just about all of it.

Boston filled him with energy and promise and a stroke of very good luck. The *Christian Science Monitor*, based in Boston, was one of the most highly regarded journals in the world. When he presented a sheaf of slightly doctored recommendations from the *Belfast News Letter*, another credited paper, they were so impressed that they quickly hired him as a roving reporter. He managed to cover his astonishment at the success of the ploy, then spent the following two years in this much enjoyed and successful occupation. A leading advertising agency, Vickers and Benson, based in Boston with branches in Chicago and Toronto, became very taken with the fluency of his writings and offered him a job as creative copywriter in their Chicago office.

He took the position and by a second stroke of good fortune met my mother to be – Vera Franklin of Durham City, a graduate of a Belgian convent. He offered his hand in marriage and then whisked her off to Toronto, where he joined the Canadian offices of Vickers and Benson.

There he produced one of the most commercially successful slogans in the soft drink industry. 7 Up, though popular, was always slightly lagging behind the leading Coca-Cola brand. He came up with the slogan, '7 Up – You'll Like It – It Likes You!' It worked, and so did my father on the basis of those two lines, solidly for the next 20 years. Somewhere during those 20 years I was born – on 28 May 1929 – 100 yards from a waterfront house in downtown Toronto. My sister Noreen followed two years later.

★ ★ ★

Back to Heathrow and my father's arrival. We hadn't seen each other in two years and clasped each other like long-lost best friends.

He had two wishes he wanted to fulfil after making sure that our marriage had the full blessings of Sheila's mother and father. One was to see his sister Maisie in Belfast, whom he hadn't seen in 40 years, and the other was to celebrate the reunion with a large frothy pint of locally brewed Guinness. He did both and, reassured that our marriage was well on track, bid us all a fond farewell, with a specially warm kiss to Sheila, and boarded his return flight to Toronto.

And so the bans were read. Canon Arthur Payton, one of the Anglican Church's most spirited orators, was asked by Sheila's mother to conduct the ceremony and gave his full blessings. One more arrangement remained. We telephoned Paul Summerville in Toronto, my original partner in The Three Deuces. He hardly paused a nanosecond before pledging his presence as Best Man. Barry Authors, who had been the tour guide and career fixer to the early Three Deuces, decided that Tiptree would be about the nicest place to spend that weekend and ticketed the seat next to Paul's.

They arrived in London just in time to pile into our little Mini van and accompany us to Soho, where we were to pick up two rented morning suits for the occasion and twin wedding rings for Sheila and me. Everything was running right according to plan, until we pulled up in front of the jewellery store in Old Compton Street. Paul and Barry tumbled out of the windowless back space of the Mini and Sheila and I stepped out of the front. I took out my wallet and was passing Sheila a sheaf of pound notes for the rings when I felt a firm hand on my shoulder, which hardly shifted as I turned around to see who or what was behind me. He was about six feet tall and with his constable's helmet gained at least another foot. He looked massive and was every inch a dedicated member of the City Constabulary.

'This kind of transaction is not at all legal, sir,' he said, 'especially in open view of the passing public. I'll need some identification, sir, if you would.'

It suddenly struck me that here was I handing over a wad of pound notes to Sheila in the middle of one of the most notorious prostitution walk-abouts in the world. I began to wonder what our chances were of adjoining cells. I gurgled an attempted explanation, as Barry gave Paul a nudge and the two of them walked to the front of the van and began looking at overhead cloud formations. Meantime the constable had removed my Canadian driver's license from the wallet.

'Canadian, eh?'

He left the rest of it hanging, as if to say, 'Well, what else do you expect?'

I didn't say anything, I was in deep enough already. But Sheila, in a no-nonsense Scots reply, had him backing up onto the kerb after explaining the situation. He at least had the courtesy to appear properly abashed as he handed back the driver's license, and even managed a small wave as we clambered back into the van.

Sheila was now into her 'last minute purchases for the wedding' agenda, deciding to take all of it back to Tiptree by train and leaving us to meet her there later in the evening. We crossed the street to a quiet corner pub, ordered three glasses of mild white wine, and toasted our escape from the law and the exciting prospects of tomorrow's ceremony.

It turned out to be a beautifully joyous occasion. The path approaching the church was lined with half the village turned out in ribboned bonnets, spats and jackets, all waving and cheering. Sheila looked a dream and Doc and Bess were in their glory. My Canadian buddies Paul and Barry were cutting up with just about everybody and, from the pulpit, the Reverend Payton's rhetoric soared to new and greater heights. The after-wedding celebrations reached such a pitch that no one wanted to leave; some in fact weren't able to. Sheila and I didn't get around to setting off on our honeymoon to Devon and Cornwall until the next morning.

After an exhilarating few days rambling around Woolacombe Bay, we drove across to Fowey and Polperro, drinking in both the land and sea beauties of Cornwall, enhanced with a few restorative drop-ins at village pubs along the way. It was with a deep sense of regret and a few backward glances that we returned to London.

Chapter Five

I had dropped off Sheila at the entrance to her office in Piccadilly, headed back to our flat and was just finishing my second coffee of the morning when the phone rang.

'This is your agent.'

'So what's happened, has the business collapsed?'

'No, in fact I've just drummed up some. I've booked an American tap dancer, Will Gaines, into *Sunday Night at the London Palladium* and I think I've got you a five-week tour of the Bailey Club circuit up north!'

'You're magnificent! Maybe we should celebrate!'

'You could take me out to dinner.'

'That would be a pleasure.'

As the popularity of Variety theatres declined, the Northern clubs moved in and established themselves as a network of highly profitable, huge-capacity entertainment rooms in the north-east and north-west, spotted in the high-density areas of Manchester, Newcastle, Doncaster, Nottingham, Sheffield and Leeds. Each had a mile-long bar, drinks just a nudge over pub prices and drew in patrons to the tune of high hundreds over the week, numbers which made most of the club owners down in the London area green with envy. They were ambitious, had a keen sense of what made a cabaret room work and we were happy to take on the five-week offer.

So I tuned up my vocal chords, recalled a few gags I'd heard during the shows in the American Forces zone and hit the Bailey

Circuit at a brisk canter. It was high-wire stuff, but I think, for the most part, I got away with it. There was a friendly star winking away in those northern skies.

In the States they talk about 'southern hospitality' – in the UK it's very much a part of the north. There were two shows a night, most always in highly talented company, and in between we visited the customer's tables, for a sip and some conversation. This began as a kind of understood obligation but changed midway through the first week to something that became more and more of a pleasure. Whichever table you stopped at, you'd find yourself invited into the company of such welcoming warmth and generosity you wondered why you'd ever balked at it. Strange thing, this fear of the unknown!

The first three weeks of the circuit tour had now drawn to a close – next up, Doncaster. The top of the bill that week was well on the way to becoming one of the greatest and most endearing stars in this magical but mysterious business. I had to admit I didn't know Les Dawson that well, really only by reputation, but the people knew him and they loved him wherever he went. Every door was open to him and he was ushered through every one of them.

Opening night, I had stopped half way down the room after finishing my 'turn', held there by a thunder-clapping outbreak of new applause; it swept the room like a tidal wave. The welcome for Les Dawson would have matched Nelson's home-coming after stopping Napoleon cold at Waterloo. I watched him jump up on stage, crash out an arpeggio at the piano and then beckon me back up with him. I still don't know how I got there, but there I was, his arm around my shoulder and whispering to me, 'Do you know 'That Old Gang of Mine'?'

Before I could stutter a reply he was into the first chorus and we sang it, this time with my arm on his shoulder, rearranging some of the lyrics but staying right along with him. Those few golden moments were worth the whole tour and it still sends ripples up my spine whenever I recall them.

Things were bound to get somewhat more subdued after that, but only temporarily. The last stop on my circuit schedule was at the City Varieties Theatre in Leeds, once a 'must' date in the heyday of Variety, where speciality acts and top-line comics and singers were booked in weekly. This week I was sharing top billing with Jean Francine, a 'Sensational Continental Strip Star' or, as she was more elegantly labelled, a Classic Tableau Artiste – a lady who this particular week was displaying the charms of Aphrodite, the Greek Goddess of Love. First the Elgin Marbles, now this!

In the 1960s, a tableau artiste was not allowed to move so much as a muscle under her silks and chiffon, let alone anything else. A sense of movement was lent to her portrayal by switching on fans in both the off-stage wings, positioned to subtly ruffle the lady's covering to suggest something other than classic undulations underneath. Anyway, it seemed to satisfy the middle-aged raincoat brigade who could be counted on to fill at least the first six rows at all performances. The audience needed me as much as a seven-foot Masai warrior needed stilts, and spent the 20 minutes of my act munching newspaper-wrapped potato chips, held discreetly in their laps.

On the third day of my detention, I received a phone call from Sheila, informing me that a company called AP Films had rung about auditioning for a new puppet TV series to follow the already established *Stingray*. The programme I had heard of, but AP Films rang not even a distant bell. So much for my instincts regarding the people and things that would have a profound impact on my life.

British Rail travel in those days was more of a hit and miss business. Maybe we should forget the 'hit' part. Anyway, planning a trip that was going to return you to the place you had started out from on the same day had a probable failure rate of 70 per cent. But after three double evening performances with Madame Francine and her 'band of audience brothers', there was nothing that would stop me from trying. The earliest train out of Leeds was at 7.00am the next morning and I was on it, clutching a folded piece of paper with

'G Anderson, The White House, Gerrards Cross' scrawled across it. I pulled into London's St Pancras Station just in time to hop aboard a Buckinghamshire train and was on my way to Gerrards Cross, wherever that was, and to G Anderson, whoever he was.

An olive-green Rover sedan picked me up at the station and ten minutes later dropped me off at the White House. Nice entrance and altogether a most impressive gabled house. I was directed to the downstairs area which was in the midst of being converted into a sound studio by a gentle, knowing and, as it turned out, most helpful sound engineer. His name was John Peverill.

He sat me down at a small table in front of a microphone, then disappeared around a corner, trailing two immensely long lengths of wire. He reappeared a minute later, this time with two pages of script, and pointed to the beginning of the dialogue on page one.

'Try the top sequence, all right?'

He gave me a thumbs-up and then retraced his steps to wherever he'd disappeared to the first time, asking me for a voice level on the way. The level okay'd and I started at the top, no character name indicated, clueless as to which role the words belonged to. So began my audition reading for *Thunderbirds*.

Fifteen minutes later, on the way back to the station, John said, 'I thought that went really well – maybe we'll be seeing you again.'

'Did you tape many try-outs today?'

'Yes,' John answered, 'quite a few. You were the last.'

Those final words of his, 'You were the last', kept repeating themselves in time to the clickety-clack of the train wheels during most of the journey back to Leeds. It had been a day of much confusion and unanswered questions, but half of life can get you like that, if you let it.

'Well, don't – just get on with it!'

There's that voice again.

'All right – so what do I do? Return to Leeds tripping the light fantastic and, on my arrival at the theatre, throw my arms around

Mme Francine and tell her that this has been one of the most rewarding weeks of my life?'

'It's worth a try.'

'Okay – maybe.' And it was.

Mme Francine took on a new glow, the theatre's first six rows were suddenly occupied by people not raincoats, and at the end I stepped off stage to the most respectful applause of the week.

★ ★ ★

I'd been back in London for just two days, following my final week's run on the Bailey circuit, and was occupied in some random plotting for the future when I was interrupted by the ringing of the telephone. It was a call from Gerrards Cross, offering me the part of Scott Tracy in *Thunderbirds*. I was in the pilot film!

I looked out the window onto a rain-drenched London that had never looked more beautiful.

The large brown manila envelope containing the *Thunderbirds* pilot script arrived by special messenger next morning. I tipped the biker far too heavily, then held the weight of it in my hands a moment or two before telephoning Sheila to tell her of the package's arrival. Next I poured out a cup of coffee, plopped down in our only easy chair and began to read.

The pilot episode was titled 'Trapped in the Sky' and was written by the producers, Gerry and Sylvia Anderson. It was a high-altitude thriller involving an atomic-powered airliner, carrying a powerful bomb hidden in the landing gear, ready to detonate the moment the wheels touched the ground. Problem – how to land without blowing the craft and everyone on board to smithereens?

There is no way of guaranteeing how a pilot TV film will fare under the scrutiny of networks and series speculators. But it was a good heart-thumping piece to head a series with and to set down a benchmark for the weekly episodes that would hopefully follow. The performances on the voice track would certainly be vital.

Three days later I entered the recording studios where *Thunderbirds* would blast off. John Peverill came up and nudged me gently in the back.

'I was pretty sure after you put down that track I'd be seeing you again.'

'I was hoping the same. Thanks.'

On the morning of the first run-through we were introduced to each other by name and playing character and then waited for the 'man'. Voice veterans Ray Barrett and David Graham had already gone some innings with the Andersons up to the last and most winning series, *Stingray*. They were recalling some of the more out-of-bounds incidents when there was a loud mike click and a voice issued from Central Control.

'Hi everybody, sorry I'm late, we'll be right in.'

The 'we' were Gerry and Sylvia Anderson, creators and producers of *Thunderbirds*, and in minutes they were threading through the bunch of us, with hellos to old colleagues Ray and David and warm welcomes to the newcomers. Minutes later we were on the starting line. Thunderbirds were GO!

I can't recall there ever being more than two multi-directional microphones at any of the recording sessions, which helped give a genuine feel of reality to the sound whether we were 40,000 miles out in space or tinkering around at ground level. But it was pretty close formation stuff – we had to keep elbows in and feet poised to move in and out of the mike field in an instant. This had certainly served the BBC Drama department well over the years, producing a sound quality that was the envy of every other broadcasting network in the world.

However, we usually managed a slip or two during the sessions, like the occasional loud flapping of a script dropping to the floor or an unrehearsed collision when one of the actors was late getting into his microphone position. A definite yellow card on that one!

It was quite a cast list that was gathered for the start of the series. Peter Dyneley was the patriarchal Jeff Tracy, with sons Virgil (David Holliday), Gordon (David Graham), John (Ray Barrett) and myself as Scott. Christine Finn was Tin-Tin, David Graham was Brains and also Parker, Sylvia Anderson was Lady Penelope and Ray Barrett was the sinister Hood. Soon after we were joined by Matt Zimmerman, as Jeff's youngest son Alan. Others, like John Tate, Paul Maxwell, Neil McCallum and Bob Monkhouse, were welcomed aboard later. Sadly, David Holliday, who originated the character Virgil, went back to work in America after the first 26 episodes so Jeremy Wilkin took over the role.

We weren't really aware that anything exceptional was going on during those early recording days. True, after the initial sessions, there seemed to be a genuine rapport building – a feeling of things coming together, a kind of rhythm there, underlying it all. Even the guest characters seemed to catch the tempo. I don't know who the drummer was, but he was laying down some fine guide tracks.

But there was little doubt as to where the majority of the minor role voices would come from, and for good reason. Compared to Aussie Ray Barrett and Eastender David Graham, the rest of us paled in comparison. Those two could reel off a string of bona-fide vocal variations that would fit skin-tight onto characters as poles apart as Ray's DJ Rick O'Shea and David's Light Fingered Fred.

Aside from my role as Scott Tracy, I'd be lucky to come up with one, and even that would be a two line 1st Reporter or a disengaged voice disappearing down an outer vortex somewhere. My minor characters wouldn't hang around that long anyway; a dozen lines or so would usually terminate their involvement in the plot. Matt Zimmerman was maybe a notch or two above me in these multi-voice stakes, but where he really shone was in the buoyancy he gave to Alan Tracy, giving him pole position among the young feminine viewers.

By comparison to us, Peter Dyneley was an old hand in voice

diversity, although he could never quite lose that deep-lying honeycomb sound that emerged with just about everything he uttered. He was, as Sylvia Anderson described him, an authentic Ernest Hemingway character whose heart, underneath that sometimes gruff exterior, beat with the warmest generosity.

So, on with the show and the possibility of a series! The voice tracks were top of the agenda. Once they were nailed, the rest could follow. Writers Dennis Spooner and Alan Fennell had already submitted follow-on scripts to the pilot film and were standing by for the go-ahead. That pilot episode of *Thunderbirds*, 'Trapped in the Sky', which had been scripted by the Andersons, was finally okayed and was now geared to go!

By the time 'Trapped' was fully edited, with titles and a complete musical score and ready for showing, eight follow-up episodes had already moved into differing stages of development. The pace of production had been full on, but now a log-jam of episodes was building and it needed clearing. An immediate showing was arranged in London with Lew Grade, probably the UK's most influential global producer, in the front row.

Gerry Anderson remembers holding his breath at the conclusion of the episode, wondering whether or not he would get an okay from Britain's most successful entertainment exporter. Grade's international clout would be critical in getting him a further foothold in the American market. He needn't have worried; he got the okay and with it a little more than he expected.

Lew Grade was on his feet as the end credits came up, exclaiming: 'A half hour's not enough – it's too good – we've got to go for the hour!'

It was quite a tribute from the ATV impresario, but now it began to dawn on all present the amount of added writing and filming that would be involved in doubling the present 25-minute programmes – expanding the current storylines, developing sub-plots for each episode and arranging hours of re-voicing. Look out – another log-jam!

Gerry Anderson and Alan Pattillo immediately dug in to bring the episodes up to the required double length – the amount of restructuring needed proved enormous. The call went out to Tony Barwick, who had spent the last few years as a computer whiz kid in Silicon Valley, California, but who had recently returned and gone back to his first love of script writing. One of his greatest off-hour delights was in devising scenarios that would appear impossible to get out of and then doing just that. He and *Thunderbirds* fitted together like hand and glove.

When Gerry's highly ambitious concept of *Thunderbirds* was born, both he and Sylvia had been well prepared for it. The seeds had been well sown through previous productions of *Supercar, Fireball XL5* and *Stingray*. They could now draw from a band of fully blooded young craftsmen who, given the right direction, could help vault *Thunderbirds* onto the top rung. That guidance was handled by associate producer Reg Hill, director of photography John Read, special effects supremo Derek Meddings and art director Bob Bell among others.

Barry Gray, who had composed the excitingly dramatic theme and incidental music for the series, was coming up with more of the same at his home studio in Dollis Hill. The combination of front office know-how and the bundles of fresh energy coming up from the studio floor was proving a near unbeatable combination in keeping pace with the new, enlarged hour-long series. But now, since there were so many added subplots flying around, our only difficulty as voice artists was in keeping straight which subplot fitted into which original storyline. Pretty interesting at times, some of those sudden re-writes!

Anyway, it must have all come together in the right places. When the series began to show, audiences loved it and the ratings zoomed. The home front looked secure and Lew Grade now had a well-credited commodity to take to the American market.

One of my most enduring recollections of *Thunderbirds* and the early recording sessions was, believe it or not, the aroma of Mars bars! AP Films had their own sound stage in one of the single-storey units that made up a large industrial estate on the outskirts of Slough. In all respects, the building and the facilities were ideal, except for one thing: a Mars bar factory which probably produced around a thousand bars a day was situated about 30 feet away from AP's front door. A single unwrapped Mars bar wouldn't have been any kind of problem, maybe quite the reverse. But with a stack of thousands, piled within 30 feet of a door that's swinging in and out most of the day, you've got a high-density permeation that would drive a sniffer dog berserk.

I haven't really been able to look at a Mars bar wrapper since. On the other hand I've gone through pots of popcorn watching old *Thunderbirds* episodes, still in awe at the punch, vision and pure entertainment they still offer after all these years, years that started back in the 1960s in that humble one-storey AP Films Studio on the Slough Trading Estate. You never get the same answer twice regarding what has made *Thunderbirds* still tick after all these years, and probably you never will. But the one thing that just about everybody is agreed upon is the great affection in which International Rescue is still held around the world.

But back on the floor, time was still at a premium, nip and tucking all the way, with the youthful tech crew, the puppeteers and the older hands of the production team synchronised at breakneck speed to bring the revamped episodes in under the wire. In an amazingly short span of time, they did it. *Thunderbirds* was back in orbit!

★ ★ ★

The voice cast was now allowed a breather. We were still a long way from the end of the series, but the voice track sessions would now be more spaced out than they had been, which gave us some room to take a look around and see what was out there.

Ray Barrett was headed for a new North Sea Oil series called *Mogul* (which later became *The Troubleshooters*), David Graham was lined up for voice-over assignments on the Daleks in *Doctor Who*, and I was making my way over to Shepperton Studios for a meeting with director James B Harris regarding a Cold War film called *The Bedford Incident*. Harris had been Kubrick's uncredited producer during pre-production on *Dr Strangelove*, where he had helped gather a brilliant cast to fill some extraordinary character roles. It looked like another intriguing line-up for this one, with Richard Widmark, Sidney Poitier, Eric Portman, Martin Balsam and Donald Sutherland. A heady mix to line up with, and a kick to be on a cast list with Donald. We arranged to meet up in the studio pub after the day's shoot and grab some Canadian beer on tap – that's if neither one of us had been tipped overboard from the *USS Bedford*'s main deck.

I located my dressing room and the naval rig hanging newly pressed in the wardrobe, ready to go; well, not quite. I counted at least 30 uniform buttons to find holes for. The crews must have spent a lot of duty time tending to the same thing. I fumbled a few but still managed enough to have myself looking presentable and ready for action. Hoping I would pass muster, I made my way down the corridor to the 'A' Stage entrance door and two-fisted it open. Wow! The sound stage was almost completely taken up, corner to corner, by a massive, studio-built replica of a US destroyer's top deck. The area was bustling with fitters and deckhands attending to all the last-minute strapping down, tightening up and securing. I skirted most of the action and was just congratulating myself on surviving the first few minutes on deck, when I walked straight into a weighty anchor chain dangling down over the deck railing.

I reeled back with the impact banging around inside my head, when a voice from behind enquired, 'Are you all right?'

I turned around to find James Harris wearing a very concerned look.

'Yes, sure, thanks,' I assured him.

Even so, I let him lead me over to one of the canvas chairs reserved for the performers. I noticed my name wasn't on any of them. He sat down alongside, scanned the preparations around the floor and then looked back to me.

'I'm afraid there won't be too many laughs on this one,' he said. 'I think it's going to be a pretty tight ship, but you'll be okay.' I thanked him for the alert as he got up to answer a beckoning First Assistant across the floor, leaving me wondering what the caution was all about. As it turned out I was grateful for it.

We had hardly cleared port, although still bounded by the four walls of the studio, when Widmark literally took command of the ship and part of the direction. On the days when his character, a fervent Yankee patriot, was in a particularly gung-ho mood, he had salutes shooting back at him with a snap that could have dislocated a wrist. Deckhands were suddenly giving him enough deck area to steer through a PT boat. Poitier meantime was the epitome of cool, keeping well removed from the aggro that threatened from time to time to spill across the deck. I took the cue and found myself a look-out post on the far railing, thinking, 'You're one hell of an actor, Richard, but I'm not sure I'll be signing on for your next one.'

Guess what, though. I did. But shucks, that was the spirit that won the West, wasn't it? That next time was in Munich in a bizarre filming situation that was a story all by itself, but all that came a few sound stages later.

★ ★ ★

Spurred on by the news that Lew Grade was making a serious bid for the North American market, major studios around London, which previously had been the preserve of feature films, were now clearing floor space for a new batch of half-hour and full hour TV adventures in a bid for overseas takers.

The first of these to come my way was being produced at the

beautiful MGM Studios at Borehamwood. It was the favourite of many actors and producers because of the in-built Hollywood glamour that surrounded it – with a retinue of such Tinsel Town names as Spencer Tracy, Robert Taylor, Ava Gardner, Elizabeth Taylor and Clark Gable, whose film posters graced most of the studio corridors. You were stepping into a tradition that was both as close as your shoulder and as far away as the firmament.

On the appointed morning, I drove through the tall brick pillars that announced the MGM Studios and was passed instructions on how to get to the production office, where I would show my wares to the director. That part I managed all right, the rest is a bit of a blur.

The series I had come to be seen about was *Danger Man*, starring Patrick McGoohan, and the episode was titled 'The Mercenaries'. On the way in I caught a glimpse of McGoohan as he passed me coming out of the office. He gave me a wink which I can only describe as very Irish. I had by chance been sitting a few tables away from him in a Swiss Cottage pub a few weeks previously as he sat in deep conversation with a striped shirt executive type. McGoohan was looking a bit shaggy then and maybe carrying a little more weight than he needed, but there was an electricity about him that attracted more than a few looks around the room. Now, on this Monday morning, he looked sleek, tanned and trim – he was *Danger Man*.

I got the part, but made no great impression as a rookie conscript. The camera was all McGoohan's and he parlayed that all the way to a hit series. But I remembered that wink, an actor's wink, and the way it dissolved the pressure that had been building inside, ever since coming through those tall brick pillars that morning.

* * *

Our first son, Damian, now decided to make his appearance, jumping the gun six weeks before his expected arrival just as we had moved into our new house on West Mersea Island, a few miles outbound from Colchester in Essex. Another celebration came 16 months later, when Ben, son number two, made his way into the family album but had the courtesy to arrive right on time. Our house was bulging and our cup did verily runneth over!

Time to stock up the pantry.

Chapter Six

Within weeks of Damian's birth, the Tracy brothers were back in their seat belts and gathered around the two main microphones at the AP Films sound studio. The session would wrap up the 26th episode of the first season's run.

I say 'first' because early reports on the showings of the series from just about everywhere looked favourable enough to predict another full series of *Thunderbirds*; it seemed a logical follow-on. But Gerry Anderson was thinking about something even further down the line. He called Lew Grade and broached him on the idea for a full-scale film production of *Thunderbirds*. The second TV series could be shot simultaneously.

Grade was sold on the idea and gave Gerry the green light to go ahead. *Thunderbirds Are Go* was under starter's orders. Then a few weeks later, Lew Grade dropped a bombshell.

From a favourable situation, where all three television companies were vying for the rights for American network distribution, things started going sour. Grade could not get agreement on the distribution deal he wanted and, when those negotiations cooled, the remaining contenders bailed out. *Thunderbirds Are Go* was still backed by a full commitment and was geared to roll under its new banner of Century 21, but the follow-up to the TV series, where it had all started, was lost in space – only six new episodes were made before the show was cancelled.

It was a major blow but there was hardly a sign of it from the studio floor. All systems went flat out – 'a thumb your nose' reply to a possibly demoralising turn of events. The TV series steered clear of the obituary columns and instead soon found a prominent place in the entertainment pages. 1965-6 saw the T-Bird insignia appearing on network screens across Europe, while at the same time syndication was being picked up on the full 32 episodes in America and Canada. Meanwhile *Thunderbirds Are Go* was out on the runway warming up for its premiere West End showing.

★ ★ ★

My next port of call was a telephone box – not your familiar 'drop 10p in the slot' kind that could link you up to any overseas service you required, but one that could actually transport you there or, if preferred, to another galaxy in the space of a second. The master space voyager was of course Doctor Who, in the 'earthly' guise of silver-haired, frock-coated William Hartnell. This particular four-part series was called 'The Gunfighters' – a story that back-stepped in time to an era almost two centuries before in America's Wild West. 'The Gunfighters' was unashamedly borrowed from an original John Sturges movie called *Gunfight at the OK Corral*, which starred Burt Lancaster and Kirk Douglas and came with a haunting, hit parade theme song, recorded by Frankie Laine.

Hartnell was a great if sometimes gruff old trouper, never known to bother too much with the niceties of introductions. He strode over, the first day, his black Stetson tilted back a little from his forehead, somewhat like a no-nonsense Dodge City sheriff.

'So you're the real thing, eh?'

Not at all sure where this was going, I shifted a degree or two out of his direct line of fire.

'What do you mean?'

'Are you from above or below the Mason Dixon line?'

The Mason Dixon line was the geographical divider between the northern and the sometimes bigoted southern American states.

'Quite a lot north,' I replied. 'Canada.'

He nodded, 'Good, that's good.' We got along quite nicely after that.

The BBC's budget, so skimpy at times you could see right through it, couldn't obviously come up with major film funds and had to settle for a band of desperadoes conscripted from the plains of Basildon, Billericay and Crouch End. The Wild Bunch they were never going to be.

At the appointed hour they rode into town, one of them urging on an animal that ambled along suspiciously like a mule, then tied up at the local saloon to take a few belts before the big confrontation. By some strange split time quirk, the establishment was bartended by David (Brains) Graham, who had possibly been given a co-ordinate misread on his latest Thunderbird mission. His brief was to take one look at the company of gunslingers coming through the swing doors and drop in a swoon behind the bar. There followed a wall-to-wall shoot-out over David's prone body, with gunslingers dropping to the floor all around him. It was probably the safest place he could have chosen.

A day or so after the saloon shoot-out – and probably while the props team was still sweeping up the shattered remains of corn whisky and sasparilla bottles, trying to make good some of the damage done to the overturned tables and chairs – I was on my way to Pinewood and a meeting with director Lewis Gilbert, who was putting together the latest 007 adventure, *You Only Live Twice*. Things were warming up.

Pinewood Studios was an even more heart-thumping first-time experience than Shepperton. After a brief introductory meeting in the 007 office, I followed director Gilbert and company, a few respectful paces behind, towards the studio bar and restaurant. The way took us along a deeply carpeted corridor and past the now obligatory gallery of stars – stars who had made Pinewood one of the top-rated studios in Europe. It was the kind of humbling experience that had you expecting one or two of them to move out of frame and ask for your credentials.

Lewis Gilbert had certainly gathered his share. He broke into the director's top tier in the 1950s with a succession of winners – *The Sea Shall Not Have Them, Reach for the Sky* and *The Admirable Crichton.* He'd brought in *Alfie* with Michael Caine just the year before – his biggest box-office hit to date. Cubby Broccoli wanted him for this one and he got him. He also secured the screen's most wildly imaginative set designer in Ken Adam, who had created the state-of-the-art sets for *Dr Strangelove.* What with Ken's towering volcano shooting a sky full of pyrotechnics on land and a tearaway nuclear rocket powering up and away into space and, of course, Sean Connery, it would prove to be the most audience-grabbing 007 production yet.

My 'pivotal' place in the film was at the control room console, seated in front of a staggering configuration of dials, buttons and gauges, appearing to have a total grasp of which one of them covered where in our space probe tracking of the auto-destruct rocket. Little wonder our side in the Space Race ran into an impasse or two.

But now other troubles were brewing in the 007 enclave. Stay tuned!

★ ★ ★

Meanwhile, news was popping from Century 21 that the Andersons had come up with another 'in space' adventure series. The concept was a notable departure from any formats produced previously – it would be titled *Captain Scarlet and the Mysterons*, head and body shapes of the puppets would now be perfectly proportioned and, just to make it a clean slate, there'd be nary a whisper of a *Thunderbirds* voice on the track. So, time then to be a touch philosophical and to count our blessings for the fine innings we'd had with *Thunderbirds* and to relish the news that Gerry and Sylvia and that happy young band of studio magicians were back again doing what they did so remarkably well.

But Century 21 wasn't quite through with me yet. During the putting together of the last *Thunderbirds* episodes, Gerry asked me to write and voice a series of intros to explain 'the story so far' when each 50-minute episode was re-edited into two 25-minute shows. This was for the newly signed American syndication where *Thunderbirds* would air in a half-hour slot. Having scripted this sort of thing in Canadian radio and TV, I happily agreed. The distributors were okay with the results and so was Century 21.

The Dirty Dozen was the kind of picture Robert Aldrich loved to make and MGM was happy that he go ahead with it. Finance on an Aldrich production was seldom a problem. Apart from Sam Peckinpah, he was about the only director around with the cojones and the talent to tackle the kind of macho manpower the story called for. But just a few weeks into the filming, he might well have wondered why he didn't just pack it in, plough up a fertile 'back forty' somewhere, breed llamas and plant a few guava orchards. The pre-shoot wrangling with studio and agents made it tough going, but Aldrich wouldn't go quietly into the night – he relished this kind of challenge and began completing his cast list.

An inventory of the 15th century Borgia family would read like a weekend cricket roster compared to the bunch he assembled for *The Dirty Dozen* – Lee Marvin, Ernest Borgnine, Charles Bronson, John Cassavetes, Robert Ryan and Telly Savalas. Genghis Khan would have run a mile, but somehow Aldrich managed to harness the combustibility of that line-up and they loved him.

I remember the film more, though, for meeting up with Donald Sutherland again and our ham-handed efforts to cart 6'5" of Clint Walker out from a wide-open target area into a more protected space under a grove of nearby poplar trees. He weighed as much as a Pittsburgh Steeler lineman and the strain of it was knee-shattering –

better we should have stayed in the line of fire and saved some tendons.

After that spot of character building and an all too brief period of convalescence, I was detailed along with my shovel to a dugout further along the line. How many times I redug that two-foot length of trench I don't know, but I must have displaced enough earth for a fair-sized underground car park. Maybe I got caught up in the desperate need for reality that Aldrich stamped on his 'go for broke' style or my inner clock went into over-drive, but I just couldn't slow down the berserk pace of the shovelling. By the end of the scene I had become a confirmed pacifist. When I finally got to view the scene at a preview, thinking it might have won me at least a BAFTA mention for outstanding courage under fire, it had just made the bottom border of the screen – not what you'd call a core part of the action.

★ ★ ★

Meantime, back at our West Mersea homestead, there was a new baby in the pipeline to join Damian. That, combined with all our train travel to and fro, made it a growing imperative to find a larger family house back in London.

Sheila, with all this progeny around her, decided to let go the agency strings to concentrate on bringing up the children. The other imperative in moving was to get ourselves closer to our philosophy studies at the School of Economic Science, which we had joined just after being married in 1963. It was a deeply fascinating pursuit, considering the three universal questions, posed since time was recorded, 'Who am I? – Where did Creation come from? – What is my part in it?' Plato declared many centuries ago that 'No man should lead an unexamined life.' The school's purpose was to continue that enquiry into the 20th century through study of ancient scriptures, philosophies and eventually the practice of meditation.

Eventually, in response to many requests from its student body,

SES opened two private schools for the daytime education of their children – St Vedast, at which Damian, being slightly older, attended, and St James, which opened its doors to Ben and Paul, his younger brothers. With those triple enrolments, work would become a top priority.

I guess it wasn't the timeliest of moves. A week after committing our signatures to the final paragraph of the house sale agreement, and having pursued all leads from the six months that might lead to some gainful employment, I came up with – nothing. My work horizon had virtually gone into cloud formation.

In those days, the payment given to most actors was lamentably low. The chances of building a nest egg were very slim – the bottom had really fallen out of everything. Actors, writers, studios, everyone was affected. To almost a man we were what is called 'resting'. It sometimes happens like that, when you least expect it and certainly when you least want it. 'Surefire' arrangements fall apart, films get shoved back and the negotiators who had never been off the phone to you were now booking flights to holiday destinations to get away from it all. It's in situations like this that you stop reading your Sunday morning horoscope in case things look as if they might get even worse.

There were two courses open. You could continue invading everybody's privacy you could think of, recalling meetings, leads or chance conversations that held even a half promise; meantime you got yourself busy doing something just to get the juices stirring again. In those days an actor's credit rating was probably on a par with a scrap yard dealer's. It hadn't been that long since they'd opened the gates to an actor's burial in a proper cemetery. The odds on being able to top up an ongoing mortgage, citing acting as your profession, were out of sight.

Cue line for a long absent friend to drop by – a much slimmer friend than I remembered from a holiday time in South Wales.

'You're looking fit,' I said to Andrew, quite lost in admiration.

'I bike to work every day, or at least I did until last week end.'

'So, what happened?'

'I was afraid my eardrums were about to perforate. The place was pretty loud!'

'Where were you working?'

'A metal pressing factory, just off the North Circular Road – so there's a job opening there if you can get hold of enough ear plugs.'

'Ah, what have you been hearing?'

'Well – that a lot of things were hanging fire at the moment.'

'I think 'braked' would be putting it a little more accurately. Could I do this job?'

'Do you have an IQ of over 40? If you want the job I'll lend you my bike.'

'That's okay – I've already got one. What's the North Circular traffic like?'

Andrew gave me a grimace. 'Sometimes I was almost glad to get back in the factory.'

'You're a great inspiration! Is there anything good about the job?'

'Sure – the pay cheque at the end of the week. It's piece work – you can do all right.'

'Are your ears getting better now?'

He cupped his hand behind an ear. 'You say something?'

'Very funny. I mean, seriously?'

'Yeah, ever since I quit.'

'I might just have to give it a try, Andrew. Thanks for the tip.'

He looked over my shoulder to Sheila standing further down the hall and waved.

'Well, you've both done me a lot of favours.'

After Andrew left, I went out and oiled up my bike.

The factory site was a low, single-storied workplace built in unpainted breezeblock, set in about a quarter acre of scrubland behind the junction of the North Circular Road and the A40 highway. As I swung around the outside of a pot hole that looked ready to take in the entire front of the bike, my ears picked up the hellish grind of metal on metal issuing from a half-open window on the side of the building.

I wheeled into the property, parked my bike near the front entrance door, then spent a minute trying to shake enough circulation back into my legs to get me to stay upright without having to lean on something. I checked the name of the factory over the door: Hoppers Sheet Metal Works. Then I took a deep breath and swung it open. That was nearly as far as I got. The noise hit me like a pulsing wall of concrete. I reeled back, grabbed onto the door handle and vowed to get on the phone to my friend Andrew as soon as I got back to Muswell Hill, if I could make it that far.

My first day had begun.

The experience of working in a sheet metal factory is one that will probably last for much longer than you might wish. Life and limb are on the edge of danger from the moment you press the 'on' button. Once you position yourself at the machine, you daren't shift a tendon, otherwise the hand guiding in the sheet metal might angle in off line and cost you a couple of fingers and probably a bottle of blood. Once you've got that right, the next thing to cope with is the barrage of sounds bouncing off the walls and ceiling, not only from the gnashing of metal on metal, but from the berserk output of three rows of high kilowatt ghetto blasters belonging to the factory hands. After the first half hour I was afraid I was going to hallucinate; after the second, I was desperately wishing I could.

Next day I brought in a smallish radio-cassette player, set it beside my machine and plugged in some earphones. I was hoping it would appear that I too was joining in the factory serenade. In fact I wasn't tuned into anything, just trying to block out the sounds coming from everywhere else. I think it probably saved my ears and certainly helped spare what was left of my sanity.

So back on my bike and a harrowing return trip on the North Circular to Muswell Hill, hoping for a following wind or at least one that wasn't hitting me directly in the face. Today's weather was coming in at a cross-angle, pushing myself and the bike into a 'death row' situation along the mid strip of the Circular's dual carriageway. I can't remember who I addressed a prayer to, but someone was listening. I arrived home, utterly spent, topped up with carbon emissions but still alive and ready to eat a buffalo.

I held my ground on the shop floor for another month and, although the weekly pay slip was a life saver, providing most of what we needed, the probability of premature dementia and a permanently impaired hearing began outweighing the takings from the daily trek to the house of horrors on Hanger Lane. Just as I was tossing around the pros and cons of bearing it for maybe another week or so the telephone rang. I limped over, reckoning it was Andrew enquiring whether I was still surviving. It was a lot better than that! At the other end of the line was Sylvia Anderson, M'Lady Penelope.

'Shane, Gerry and I were both taken with the work you did on the *Thunderbirds* syndication showings in America. Sorry we didn't thank you at the time but we would now like to commission you to write a script for *Captain Scarlet*. Is that all right?'

'Sylvia, I can't possibly tell you how all right it is.'

'We're so glad. The script editor, Tony Barwick, will be calling you. By the way, the story is titled 'Avalanche'. Good luck!'

I put the phone down hoping that I'd kept most of the tremors out of my voice.

Well – still alive and now a script commission. How much more good luck could I handle in one day?

Tony Barwick phoned through the next morning.

'Nice bit of news, eh?'

'Wonderful – is this okay with you?'

'Absolutely!'

Tony, who had been a major writer for the *Thunderbirds* series, had become a good friend and golfing buddy. Neither of us burned up the course, but each round was a pleasure, even with the trail of

WORLD FAMOUS
RKO
PALACE

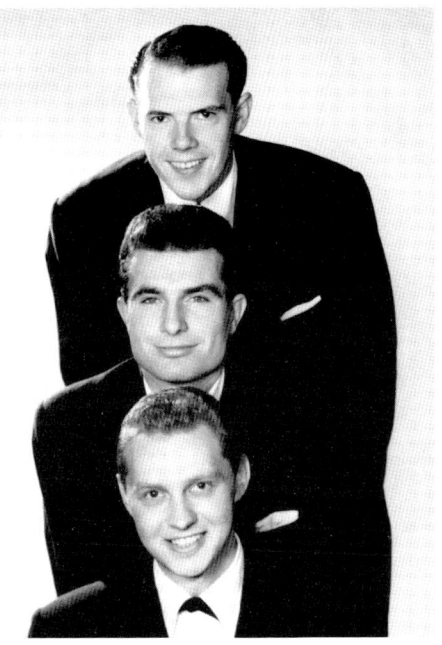

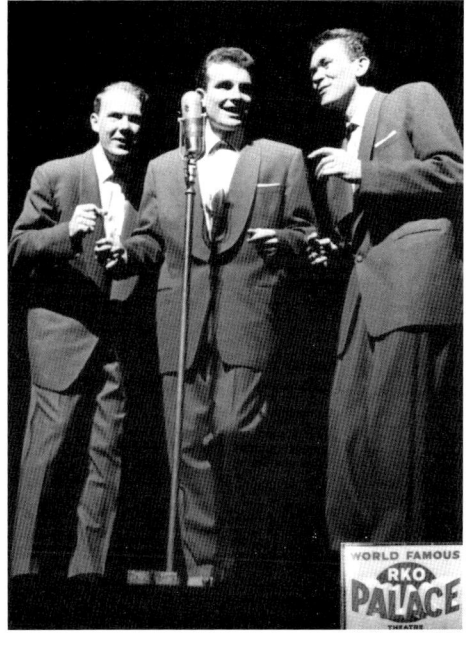

The original Three Deuces – Paul (top), me and Johnny.

Following Judy Garland into New York's Palace Theatre, with new member Barry Hamilton (right).

Sheet music of The Three Deuces' first record.

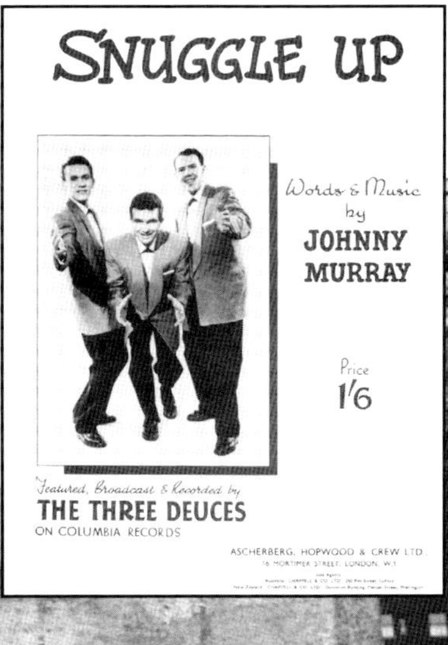
SNUGGLE UP
Words & Music
by
JOHNNY
MURRAY
Price
1/6
Featured, Broadcast & Recorded by
THE THREE DEUCES
ON COLUMBIA RECORDS
ASCHERBERG, HOPWOOD & CREW LTD.
16 MORTIMER STREET, LONDON, W.1

Taking a breather in New York on CBC's *Come Fly With Me*.

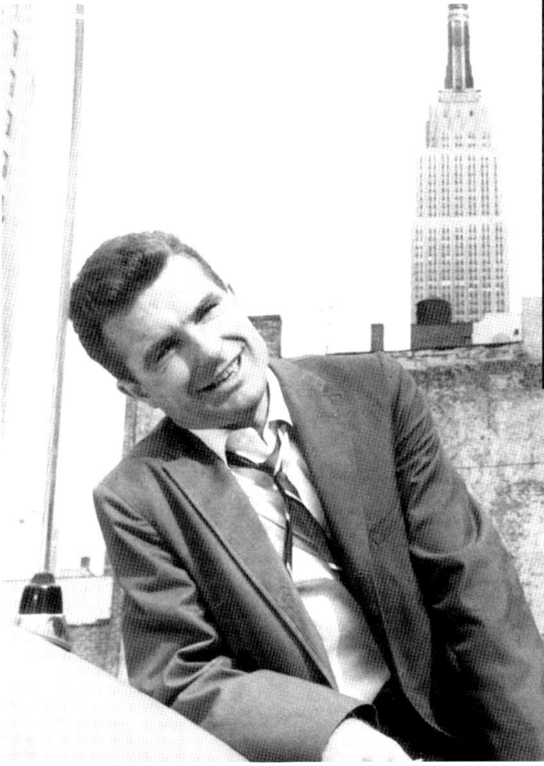

Authors and Swinson, stars at the Palladium.

Come Fly With Me takes to the air again with another adieu to Mum.

My Austin-Healey Sprite, courtesy of the TrainCo Agency.

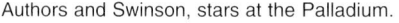

Singing for my supper in clubland.

The original Three Martinis –
Isobel, Sheila and Heather.

As Little Chief Running Bear
in *Flaming Frontier*.

As co-pilot Ace
in *Dr Strangelove*.

A head office confrontation
with Robert Flemyng in *Compact*.

Wedding bells
for Sheila and me
in Tiptree.

Scott Tracy
at the controls of
Thunderbird 1.

Rehearsing *Doctor Who*'s 'The Gunfighters' serial at Shepherd's Bush –
(left to right) Sheena Marshe (Kate), David Cole (Billy Clanton), William Hartnell (Doctor Who),
William Hurndall (Ike Clanton), me (Seth Harper) and Maurice Good (Phineas Clanton).

In *Coronation Street* with Pat Phoenix,
the queen of all she surveyed.

The first episode of *UFO*.
Thanks for the shades, Ed – I can't see a thing.

The likely lads – our sons, Damian, Ben and Paul.

As Zeke Daley with Nyree Dawn Porter as the Contessa di Contini in *The Protectors*.

Playing Zeke's blues in *The Protectors*.

On location in Munich as coach Ace Logan in *Rollerball*.

In Santa Cruz de la Palma with Sheila for *The People That Time Forgot*.

divots we gouged out of the fairways.

'Keeping fit?' he asked.

My eyes went to the bicycle parked inside the front door.

'Yes, one way or the other.'

'Okay, a biker will drop the storyline over to you in about an hour. Take today and tomorrow and see how you'd go about filling it in. You free for the rest of the week?'

'As a bird,' I answered.

So, the department heads, including Tony, were now at their starting blocks. *Captain Scarlet* was revving up. The biker delivered the story line for the 'Avalanche' episode, which gave me 24 hours to work out how it could best be developed into a first draft treatment.

Captain Scarlet, Captain Blue, Cloudbase, Captain Black, the Mysterons and a land-fall disaster – it was a heavy mix to juggle with and the timer was already ticking. If it didn't work, that's about as far as I'd get. I was hoping to turn that corner.

Francis Matthews and Ed Bishop had been drafted in as Captains Scarlet and Blue – I knew their work well, and visualising them playing the roles helped in putting down the lines the way they would say them.

I phoned the foreman of the sheet metal factory with an apology that I'd pressed my last sheet of steel. He accepted the news gracefully.

'Well, you didn't do badly, but I never really thought you were going to make it a lifetime career. I'll send what's owing on to you. Good luck.'

I spent that afternoon and most of the next day immersed in the script outline of 'Avalanche', gulping down a dozen cups of coffee before coming up with what I reckoned would be one or two workable story developments that avoided stepping on the toes of the series concept or any of the main characters.

Two days later I sat across from Tony Barwick, wearing his script editor's hat as he leafed through the pages I'd brought in, trying to hold down my heartbeat from popping up through the top of my skull. He would have made a great poker player; not a hint of what he was thinking showed on his face. But he made a better script editor, putting certain strands of a storyline on hold while moving others into areas where they could be more freely developed, and lastly returning to those abandoned strands to gather them up and meld them into a smoothly worked conclusion. It was a training session I would refer back to many times in the future, following his Don Quixote lead like a respectful Sancho Panza, even contributing enough to make it a near-collaborative effort by the end of our work day. He slid the pages back across the desk.

'Okay, the first draft is yours. Now how about some golf on Thursday?'

It was turning into a golden morning.

Tony and I both belonged to the Stage Golfing Society, an expanding group of golfers composed of film, television and theatre actors, writers and directors, wholly dedicated to getting as much time on the golf course as we could possibly get away with. For a minimal yearly subscription we were given access to championship courses at Moor Park and private courses at Richmond, Wimbledon Park and Foxhills, Surrey.

Sean Connery, who was probably solvent enough by that time to put down a covering bid on any of them, was quite content to be listed in the standard membership category, although his game was closer to par figures than most others. The society was a great fellowship and provided all who were lucky enough to get on the members' roster with some spectacular moments during the regular 18-hole play – and possibly even more memorable ones at the following 19th inside the clubhouse. The door opened on a bar at just the right height to rest a creaky elbow while sampling a commiserating drink, or even a winner's one, as you figured out how soon you'd be able to wangle another afternoon to take on the course again.

★ ★ ★

Meantime, the much-anticipated premiere of *Thunderbirds Are Go* had taken place in London's West End. Insider reports had forecast the film doing bumper business – certainly United Artists, the Hollywood distributor whose representatives had flown over for the opening, were full of expectations. If the hordes of fans that crammed Leicester Square were any indication of the film's potential box-office, Century 21 was on to a winner.

Unfortunately, it didn't quite turn out that way. The premiere, with all its hoopla and column space, exceeded expectations, but when the film went on release throughout the country it raised only a fraction of the forecast takings. Why? Nobody could come up with an answer – hopes at Century 21 zeroed. *Thunderbirds Are Go*, unhappily, just didn't!

It so stunned the United Artists people, who would have bet their collective Brooks Brothers wardrobe on it being a knock-out success, that they immediately backed the Andersons for a follow-on film – that would hopefully wipe out the failure of *Thunderbirds Are Go* and restore some of their lost credibility. So the call went out and the T-Bird voice contingent reported back in, all except for Ray Barrett who had played the villainous Hood with such satanic relish. He had flown back to Australia and decided to sit this particular summons out and hang on there a while longer. This next Anderson/United Artists co-operative venture would be named *Thunderbird 6*.

It was another fine-tuned Anderson script and we delivered it with everything we had, but with nobody thinking out loud about what the chances might be. We finalised the voice tracks, marked time during an unexplained holding delay, then trooped to our seats for the Leicester Square Odeon premiere. *Thunderbird 6* soared beautifully from take-off, executed some spectacular passes overhead, then – alas, like its predecessor – failed to maintain the flight level on provincial release. Tough old game this, eh?

Back with *Captain Scarlet*, 'Avalanche' went into its final draft some weeks later. Two more storylines were now in preparation –

'Expo 2068' and 'Inferno' followed onto my desk, which more or less took care of '67.

Walking the golf course one day, Tony and I came up with an idea for a thriller novel with a golfing background. Needless to say, it required many more hours of research on the golf course, a cross we bore with great staunchness. The book was called *Dogleg*, a term used to describe a fairway so constructed that, from the tee-off, the golfer is unable to see the green. He is virtually shooting blind. His first shot is played to gain an approach position from which the green, the target, becomes visible and thus playable. And that is how we constructed the plot of our mystery in order to nail the culprit.

Well, we completed the book, played about 20 rounds of golf between pages, tried our damnedest to get it published, but never did. But what we did succeed in doing later was to develop a film script from the book and sell the rights through my old buddy from the variety theatre days, Barry Authors, who had since moved into film production. A few years on and Telly Savalas, riding the crest of *Kojak* and in London on another project, got so taken with one of the main characters that he sat down with us to discuss taking part. Unfortunately he passed on before we could proceed further and the project was put into limbo. I still have the book though, the rights carry an 'available' option along with the lollipop man's stamp of approval – if anyone wants to have a swing.

It was while working on the book with Tony that I began hearing rumours of a possible new Century 21 series, this time starring a nine-year-old techno whiz-kid called Joe 90. If true, it was a quite different series concept from anything Gerry Anderson had previously created. I was certainly intrigued as to how they would centre a series around a character who hadn't even reached his teens yet, but since the report was scanty and certainly not official, I filed it away under 'dig for more later'.

Next day I was due at the farmhouse to have another bash at the book, noticing as I made for the kitchen that Tony appeared a little preoccupied. As I was reaching for my coffee, he handed me a typed sheet of paper which looked vaguely like some sort of contract.

'What's this?' I asked. 'How we divide the spoils of the book that we're not even half way through yet?'

'No, it's got nothing to do with the book – have a read.'

He had that enigmatic kind of smile on his face that I was always light years away from deciphering. I took a swallow of coffee and started at the top. It turned out to be a contractual offer to write two scripts for, guess what? *Joe 90*.

'But I don't even know what the series is about.'

'It's Gerry's concept – I'm on as script editor. Sorry I didn't let you know anything, but it's been kept under wraps. It'll probably mean we'll have to leave the book a while.'

'That's okay, I was getting a little confused with the plot anyway,' I said. 'But maybe you'd better tell me something about *Joe 90*.'

And so he did. Nine-year-old Joe McClaine lives with an affable but rather eccentric foster father named Mac who spends a lot of his time inventing things. His latest is something rather special. He names it BIG RAT – Brain Impulse Galvanoscope Record and Transfer. It's able to record one person's brain patterns and then programme them into someone else's. A friend in the Intelligence Service, seeing its 'intelligence' potential and despite Mac's protests, enrols Joe with the aid of the BIG RAT to become a 'most special agent'.

The first tricky item in writing the stories was to really see things through the eyes of a nine-year-old boy; the second was that the nine-year-old boy was probably a lot smarter than you were. It was a double-edged sword, one of them serrated – but maybe I never grew up that much anyway.

After the first two TV scripts had passed the first-draft hurdle to be produced and transmitted, there followed the promise of four more. Then Alan Fennell, in his off-script capacity as editor of Century 21's comic magazines, invited me to his Fleet Street office in the heart of the newspaper world, to see if I would be interested in writing some *Joe 90* comic strip episodes. I'd become very drawn to the character over the course of writing two scripts about him and the idea of setting him in another medium was a fetching one. We sealed the arrangement in a Fleet Street pub over a bottle each of the finest dark Guinness.

A few weeks on and *Joe 90* was taking to his new-found environment very comfortably and so lived to fight the good fight down another avenue. Me, I just loved walking around Fleet Street at any time of the day, breathing in the same air as some of the finest pen men around.

★ ★ ★

Five comic strip stories and six *Joe 90* TV scripts later, a call came through from *Coronation Street*. The series had now attained almost institutional status – a must-see, twice-weekly stop-in to keep up to date on the 'street', the inhabitants and all they were up to. The stars were legendary and most of them could afford to live like it. Pat Phoenix, Violet Carson, Bill Kenwright, Julie Goodyear and William Roache were some of those on the most sought after list for big gala openings and first night celebrations. It was quite a select club I was moving into.

Manchester had always been a happy stop-over since touring with The Three Deuces and then, later, fitting into occasional dramas for Granada Television. The first thing to be organised was where I was going to stay. With the Deuces we would bunk in at one of the most renowned 'artistes' digs in Manchester. The landlady's name was Alma and her home away from home was on Daisy Street.

It was such a massive house it allowed Alma to run the place in two separate halves. The left side for those appearing in legitimate theatre, the right for those playing at the lesser level of clubs and variety. By the time I returned for the *Coronation Street* run, she had lowered the bar to allow even TV performers to enter on the left. But whether you'd been booked into either the left or the right of the main stairs, that's where you stayed and any get-togethers were kept within the house boundaries. But she was a genial and generous hostess, as long as you didn't arrive after the gong for supper.

Any apprehensions I had about joining the elite of the *Street* melted after the first ten minutes of my opening rehearsal. The cast, like that of *Compact*, had that warm 'come on in' spirit that held the door wide open for all newcomers. On many an evening, after a long studio day trying to get our lines in place, we'd head for the Stables, a Granada-only members club dangerously close by.

Here, Michael Parkinson first introduced me to Jeremy Beadle, then working as a researcher for a string of top Granada dramas and documentaries. He appointed himself my unofficial guide to some of Manchester's most appealing and sometimes less appealing night spots. With Jeremy you never knew where you were headed, but I couldn't have tagged on to a more entertaining or surprise-a-minute companion.

One early evening he called by in a cab, unusual for him.

'I know, like me, you don't fancy pub visits too much,' he said, 'but this one's a bit different.'

The taxi pulled up not far from the Granada Studios at a pub called the Brown Bear. The drab brownstone front looked as if it had weathered at least a century of real Lancashire weather and hadn't come out of it all that well.

'You like English football?' Jeremy asked.

'More and more,' I answered.

'Let's go in,' he said and steered me towards the entrance.

What illumination there was inside was provided by a few large vintage globes over the bar, and others high on the walls. Otherwise the room was just a shade lighter than the evening we'd left outside. I guess that didn't matter too much – nobody was reading anything.

'So what's up?' I asked.

He nodded towards a corner where a group of drinkers were gathered around a table, all eyes turned towards a dark, tousle-haired youth sporting a Beatles hair cut. As we looked on, George Best checked his watch, eased back from the table, shook a few hands and, accompanied by one of his companions, headed for the door.

I nudged Jeremy in the ribs. 'That's him, isn't it? It's George Best!'

As he passed the bar he saw Jeremy, gave him a smile and a half wave. Jeremy waved back and then said to me, 'Must be close to curfew. We'll catch him next time.'

'Is there anybody in this city you don't know?' I asked him as we turned to the bar and ordered our drinks.

During all my months on the series (which extended, on and off, from August 1968 to December 1970), I was never aware of any under-the-table rivalry or backbiting among members of the cast. There were more than a few off-screen capers that had some of the writers salivating to include them in their more adventurous storylines, but the cast, a feisty lot when roused, would have gone walkabout if anything even remotely like an exposé got into the script – the proposition was always a non-starter.

Meantime, my character, Joe Donelli, was getting more deeply involved in the plot by the week. When the marriage of Steve and Elsie Tanner (Paul Maxwell and Pat Phoenix) was tragically cut short by Steve's suspicious death, Joe, supposedly a longtime friend, was on the run after being charged with his murder. Joe found sanctuary in Minnie Caldwell's flat and held Stan Ogden, a veteran 'street' resident, as hostage. When the police cordoned off the building – and realising the game was now up – Joe ordered Minnie to leave, then put a gun to his head and blew his brains out.

Just as well. I was hardly alive anyway, having had a heavy asthmatic reaction to those dozen cats creeping around the place.

Chapter Seven

At first glance, the pairing of Roger Moore and Tony Curtis as co-stars in an hour-long TV series titled *The Persuaders!* and scheduled for 24 episodes was, to put it mildly, a long shot – maybe 100-1. Although both were successful, attractive, charming and could deliver a flip comic line with absolute ease, their acting styles and personae were half a world apart.

Curtis was well used to the rough and tumble of New York and Hollywood movie life. When he played the hustling press agent in *Sweet Smell of Success* he was working his own kind of territory – he was a hustler, he lived, talked and thought like one and delivered the role with consummate conviction. Moore, if he had travelled those same streets, would have done so from the back seat of a chauffeur-driven Bentley. What made the partnership work, I think, was the very genuine respect each had for the other. I certainly picked that up in the scenes I acted with them. Stars can either add or subtract from the working atmosphere of a production – Roger Moore and Tony Curtis helped out everybody without reservation.

Tony Barwick was the scriptwriter on the *Persuaders!* episode I'd signed on for and drove out to the location one morning bringing me greetings from Gerry Anderson and a scriptwriting offer. The new series, now well into pre-production, would be titled *The Protectors* and would star Robert Vaughn. Gerry was in negotiations with Curtis's agent to have him play the guest lead in one of the episodes and since I was at the moment working with him – could I come in and discuss writing that particular episode for the series?

'Okay Gerry – see you there.'

It was nearly two years since my previous spin around the Andersons' universe. After *Joe 90* and a script on a golfing theme for *The Secret Service*, the last of their puppet series, I had been seconded into *UFO*. This, the Andersons' first live-action TV series, centred around the operations of SHADO – 'Supreme Headquarters Alien Defence Organisation', a secret defence network with its headquarters located 80 feet below the 'Harlington-Straker Film Studios'. The actual episodes would be filmed at the ATV Elstree and MGM Studios in Borehamwood and later at Pinewood. Intelligence funding for the organisation was drawn from a reconnaissance satellite called SID – 'Space Intruder Detector'. The whole show was run by one of the partners of the studio, Ed Straker – played by a longtime friend and role rival of mine, Ed Bishop.

I walked into the underground set and found him in his office.

'Have I still got clearance around here, Ed?'

He came around the desk, his hand extended.

'Any time you like.'

It was over a year since we'd seen each other, but that's the way it was in the actor's world; time gaps meant very little and you just picked up from where you were. Ed and I had worked together many times, in films, on stage, in TV and radio, which was his forte. His radio drama credits would fill two pages. But what I remember most about Ed was his self-appointed position as a kind of 'listening post' for the entire North American acting community in London. If a role came up that he judged was right for a particular actor, he'd be on the phone to get them to hustle over there and try out. He got more actors more jobs than anybody else, sometimes even opting out of possible selection himself.

Back to the series. For the first episode, 'Identified', I was Lieutenant Bill Johnson, co-pilot on a Seagull X-Ray aircraft under attack by a UFO. In the second, 'Computer Affair', I became a fully suited and helmeted alien wandering through the woods after the downing of his alien ship. My breathing began to accelerate as soon as I felt the last nut being tightened to secure the space helmet – in just seconds, it seemed, the visor was covered in mist and my sight range went down to about six inches. I was now coming into an asthma attack, a virtual pinball, charging into bushes, ricocheting from one tree to another, a prisoner inside my own damn suit.

The camera crew finally woke up to the fact that I had gone completely off course, and director David Lane shouted out 'Cut!', followed by the blissful sound of wrenches unlatching the holding mechanism of the space helmet. Immediately on being released, I dropped spreadeagled onto the ground, not being able to remember ever breathing so deeply before. On the way out, I passed Lane and the camera boys and flipped over my helmet into the midst of them.

'Next time, one of you lot get inside that!'

★ ★ ★

It was still early days when I received the beginnings of the *Protectors* storyline from Gerry's Group Three production office and started to work. With all the darting around between acting and writing, life was full. Things seemed to be moving nicely and I wasn't about to move out of the way.

'Zeke's Blues' would be the title of the Tony Curtis episode, in which he was to play the role of an American lounge pianist and longtime friend of Harry Rule's (the latter played by Robert Vaughn). He had flown into London for a booking in one of the West End's plushier night spots and invited Harry down for a get-together. Harry would come by, arm in arm with the Contessa, his elegant Rome operative played entrancingly by Nyree Dawn Porter, and unknowingly land them both in another sticky adventure.

To help me with my *Protectors* script, I had spent my last few days on *The Persuaders!* following Curtis' performance closely, marking the way he moved – that eye-catching style, disarming on the surface but with more than a hint of something a lot tougher underneath. I was sitting by the side of the set, jotting down a few notes, when I saw him split from Roger and come over, looking pointedly at the notebook I was using.

'Writing your memoirs?'

'No, not yet,' I laughed. '*The Protectors* production outfit asked me to write an episode for them. I think they might have approached your people about it.'

'Yeah – I heard. And you're doing the script?'

His eyes flicked back to the notebook – maybe holding a question.

'Yes, I was just watching the way you do things – thought it might help with the story – hope you don't mind?'

That seemed to clear things – there was no question in his eyes now.

'No, it's okay – so maybe I'd better think of doing it.'

Hometown Hollywood was a hotbed of gossip and innuendo, a lot of it contributed by members of its own industry. Stars learned early to keep a wary eye and who could blame them?

I got back the suggested changes and additions for the *Protectors* first draft treatment, spent a week integrating them, then hopped back to Elstree Studios and the Group Three production office to see if the script was still a runner or whether more surgery would be needed. Ever walked into a room where there was something hanging in the air so palpable you felt that one more step would be one too many? That's the way it was on that Tuesday morning. I had an uneasy feeling that 'Zeke's Blues' was in trouble – so I asked from the doorway.

'Have we got trouble with the script?'

'The script looks good and Zeke's character is fine.'

I breathed a sigh of relief that could be heard across the room.

'But there is a problem – Curtis can't do it!'

'He doesn't like the idea?'

'No, it's not that. They've shifted a shooting schedule of his out in LA. Curtis and company have begged off.'

It was disheartening news, but at least it wasn't because of the script.

'So now you're going to have to find somebody else ?'

'Yes – but I think we have … you!'

'But it wasn't written for me. I…'

'You're the logical one to do it – and we're in a tight spot.'

I protested a little more strongly, but admittedly not at top range. Zeke's role had been written, installing as much of Tony Curtis' natural appeal as I remembered noting on set. There was a character within a character involved here.

So, now what? Maybe just get on with it! There's that damn voice again!

Ray Lonnen, who played the silver-tongued 'nasty' in the episode, graciously sent along a video of it some time later and I think maybe we did okay with it. But I remember thinking more than a few times through the shoot – all right, the lead character and the script are OK, but is this how Tony Curtis would be playing it?

Aye, there indeed was the rub.

★ ★ ★

Scorpio, the Michael Winner film in which I found myself cast as a front-line government agent, looked unlikely to make the top ten of the year in spite of the acting talent Winner had gathered – Burt Lancaster as a CIA operative with a suspect double side to him, plus Alain Delon and Paul Scofield, weaving patterns that would make it doubly difficult to pin down who exactly was who. Some pretty heavy artillery there. Whether they would find the range or not was a large question.

I got a hint of how things were going as I entered into my second day's shooting. I caught the look of anguish on the face of one of

Winner's young assistants as he handed me a page of the day's rewrites. He accompanied that with a finger placed to pursed lips and said, 'Walk softly.'

The atmosphere on a film floor gets everywhere, you can't hide it. When it's good, it's electric and draws the best out of everybody. When it's not, you're walking around in ten-league boots. It gets tiring. Everything takes more time than it should, tempers go to the edge, things like klieg lights get dropped or kicked over, power-plugs malfunction and water coolers run dry. Nobody seems to know a way out of it, including the director.

Burt Lancaster, who up to now had been a warmly affable member of the cast, was now sitting apart, possibly mulling over the latest American media speculation on his private life. Alain Delon, whose exploits had taken up more tabloid space than a dozen other Gallic performers, seemed content to let things unravel the way they would.

Communications were at a bare minimum and the director seemed powerless to do anything about it. It called for a desperate measure, and unfortunately Michael Winner chose the wrong one. He headed straight for the cinematographer – who had shot half a dozen of Winner's previous films – and, in front of the entire company, dressed him down over a totally irrelevant incident. The man was devastated; he crumbled, tears in his eyes. The film never really got back on its feet after that. 'Winner' was anything but on this outing.

With another espionage scenario in view, I met up with director Irvin Kershner on a sun-filled London day in March 1974 for a part in a CIA-KGB Cold War spoof called *S*P*Y*S*. Although written as a comedy, the circumstances of the Cold War situation that prompted it were anything but. Heading into the 1950s, both the US and Russia were engaged in massive armament build-ups. It finally dawned on them that the next step taken by either one could and probably would obliterate the known world. So the earth was put on hold while these two major powers tried to figure out how to get free of the corners they'd boxed themselves into. After going through almost 20 years of it, the rest of the world had had enough. Maybe this was the value of *S*P*Y*S*, to show the absurdity of it all, even in the highest places.

It was a brave stroke on the part of the producers to bring Donald Sutherland and Elliott Gould back together again. I think they probably had some palpitations about it, hoping that Irvin Kershner would have the inner armament and the outward calm to handle what could well be an explosive mix. In truth, it wasn't that easy a shoot.

The three of us, Donald, Elliot and myself as CIA operatives, spent a major segment of the story being chased through the rain-soaked streets of Paris by a Kruschev lookalike, Kenneth J Warren. When we weren't slogging through mud up to our shins and getting shot at, we were splashing through the puddled alleyways of the Left Bank and ducking into pensione doorways to avoid being cornered by a hit squad of KGB assassins and shipped out somewhere eastward. But this was Paris and Paris is such a make-believe kind of city that it sometimes allows the line between the real and the imaginary to blur. But there were enough high-speed car incidents and wild auto chases going on through city streets to probably lock us up in the Bastille for months.

My role was that of CIA field agent Hessler, who almost ended up in analysis as each further intrigue became even more 'classified' than the one before. In fact, it became very confusing as to who he was really working for. In one scene set in a country church, I was doing a 'road runner' scramble between the offertory table and the main pulpit on my knees, trying to escape the clutches of the CIA and the KGB, not being really sure which of them was which. I came out of it with both knees torn out of a beautifully tailored Parisian suit and a heartbeat of around 190 to the minute.

It was the kind of film that knitted together well in some places and probably missed by miles on others. I don't know how the film was publicly rated, but for me it was a delight to be around Elliott Gould and Don Sutherland, working so easily in tandem again. It was almost as much fun recounting it all, back in the soft-lit safety of the hotel lounge that night.

One scene remains starkly printed on my mind. Rémy Julienne, the stunt driver from *The Italian Job*, hired for *S*P*Y*S*, engineered a crash in a getaway car through a low-topped steel gate, which ripped off the roof of the partly cut-through top of the car and would have done the same to the driver, if he hadn't ducked his head a second before the impact. He had brought his 12-year-old son along in case it was their last get-together. That night back at the hotel, we forgot all our other narrow escapes during the film and instead toasted our daredevil driver Rémy, with a round of cast applause and beaucoup de champagne.

★ ★ ★

Then it was a fond adieu to Paris and on to London. Eurostar would have been the preferred way back, but nobody had thought about building it yet. Six weeks was a long time away, even in the midst of one of the most charming cities in the world. But I was longing to get back to the family again, to be walking through fields and along country lanes with Sheila and the boys and then maybe motoring up the A1 to the Barwick farmhouse to conjure up some further twists to the plot of *Dogleg*.

We managed to get our few days in the open air, trekking the woods and the county's back trails, despite occasional squawks from the youngsters about everything from shin splints to pulled hamstrings, parts that none of them had even developed yet. But my heart went out to them – they'd marched along with true grit and, although it had been a fine family get-together, on a discomfort scale of one to ten we got well past midway. Despite trying to convince myself that night that a few more hours tomorrow might cap it off nicely, the thought of more miles to trudge was like weighing up the prospects of a cart ride to Newgate prison.

When the call came in from Pinewood next morning to come along to a meeting, we all heaved an immense 'whew' of relief. With me out of the way there'd be no family circuit training that day.

The call was for a meeting with Norman Jewison – an unexpected get-together about a project called *Rollerball*. But what it was about I hadn't a clue. Whatever, it would be a pleasure seeing him again. It had been a long time.

He had risen spectacularly through the ranks of television directors in Canada's CBC network, had expanded his reputation to New York, producing a number of primetime TV spectaculars, then continued his migration southward to the west coast and the Hollywood Hills. He must have found it to his liking – he just couldn't stop making hit movies. There were a flock of others but high on his merit list were *The Cincinnati Kid*, his first outing with Steve McQueen, *In the Heat of the Night* with Rod Steiger and Sidney Poitier, and back with McQueen for *The Thomas Crown Affair*. You can't do a great deal better than that and I've just about run out of garlands to toss at him. Oh, one more. He had now re-based himself in his home town of Toronto and opened up a Film School which was thriving.

I'd met up with him when The Three Deuces had returned to Toronto in the late 1960s for an outdoor stadium show which earned a follow-up booking on his cross-Canada TV network extravaganza. It was the usual highly rated Jewison mix of pace and panache, and the utmost pleasure to do.

Now I was walking down Pinewood's star portraits gallery once again, by this time getting quite comfortable with them all, even managing a few nods and 'hellos' on the way to the staircase that led up to Jewison's office. I was greeted at the entrance by his PA and then shown into the inner office, where Norman was sitting behind a massive period desk, piled across with sheaves of papers and enough photos to cover at least two walls. He got up immediately and extended his hand in a warm, strong handshake, then motioned me to grab a seat. As I settled in the chair by the side of his desk watching him, I couldn't help thinking what a vital kind of man he was and how he hadn't lost an iota of it over the years. He gave me a thorough look over, then sat back.

'Don't worry, I don't need you to read. Just wanted to see that you were still in one piece.'

'Do I pass?'

'Looks like it. Still singing?'

'Not so much now.'

'Maybe it's just as well – there'll be a lot of shouting on this one. It's going to be pretty violent – about a new sport called Rollerball and you'll be right in the middle of it. I'd like you to play Jimmy Caan's coach on the Houston team.'

That gave me the opportunity to reflect on what was on the line here. I'd been a pretty fair roller hockey player as a kid, but that was three decades past on Toronto side streets.

'Well, as long as I don't have to strap on the skates and buzz around the track myself – it sounds great.'

'You'll be all right. You won't have to move out of the centre circle of the track – and it's barricaded like Fort Knox.'

Norman was someone who could never resist a challenge, whether it was mounting a film full of controversy or finding the players needed to play it. The last time I'd seen James Caan was in *The Godfather Part II* – if the film was a tough one, he'd be right at home.

'Where are you shooting it?' I asked.

'Just outside Munich, in the Olympic Village.'

'Isn't that where … ?' There was a pause.

'Yes – where eleven Israeli athletes were murdered two years ago.'

A week later two Volkswagen buses carrying some of the actors and crew members drove through the gates of what was once the Olympic Village and pulled up in front of the main entrance. We turned to the windows and looked out on a slice of history – a sombre one. What should have been a celebration of a world united had been turned into an ultimate monument of hate.

The driver left his seat, came around and quietly slid back the side door. We paused, then stepped out and looked around us. Except for a few overalled cleaners and sweepers, the place appeared deserted. Over and beyond the wide stone entrance-way, we could see the semi-circular bank of grey-toned apartment blocks, constructed for the hundreds of athletes who had gathered here to compete in the 1972 Olympics. That had all happened nearly two years before, yet standing where we were, there was still more than a hint of something in the air – elusive, almost indefinable, disturbing and very much a part of the surroundings in which we stood.

Ahead, the driver beckoned us on. We collected ourselves and followed him through the stadium and into the main concourse that divided a succession of gymnasia and exercise rooms on either side, each of which, we were told, had a replica built on the floor directly below for further workouts and practice sessions.

Rollerball would be filmed in an arena further on down that had housed the original bicycle speed track. Already steeply graded, it had now been made even steeper and faster by superimposing another track on top of it. The Rollerballers would be cruising at around 40 to 50 miles per hour to capture a spinning metal ball circling high on the track. A dip of a foot would add another five mph on top of that. The players had been recruited from Roller Derby teams in New York, Los Angeles and Chicago and they were the best on the circuit. But how they would cope with the sheer grading of the track, after racing all their careers on the flat, was a large and still unanswered question.

Next morning they were on the track at 8.00am finding out. For the next two days there were spills, collisions, pile-ups, a few punch-ups, a lot of sprains and some broken bones. A few quit, but most stayed on and by the day following they were starting to get it – they were finding the balance and the pace. Collisions continued due to the quicksilver shifts in track speed but there was some spectacular roller-wheeling going on out there. It was starting to jell and Norman was beaming.

That smile broadened even more when he watched James Caan on track for the first time the next day. Caan had apparently gone through some intensive skating workouts on a roller track in LA and was handling the dips and swerves almost like a professional.

That phase of the shoot now dropping into place, I turned my thoughts to the two gung-ho confrontational scenes I had with Caan, which were coming up the next week. Head coach and star player – there could be no backing down.

James Caan had come out of almost nowhere to bag the major role of Sonny in *The Godfather*, and joined up with some firmly competitive company – Al Pacino, Robert Duvall and, of course, Marlon Brando – and he'd managed to hold his own. At times he showed the kind of combustible energy that could outpace a fire engine. I was hoping he wouldn't just blow me away in our scenes, but I needn't have worried. Caan was as generous as he was committed. We got the first encounter wrapped up in three takes. It was powerful stuff and mostly ad-lib, which Jewison was a little concerned about. But Caan argued for it and it stayed in.

During the later stages of the filming, a consortium from New York representing a large Sports Media conglomerate visited the set with the aim of buying the rights to the game in order to promote a coast-to-coast Rollerball League in the States. Norman, who had first seen the story of *Rollerball* in *Esquire* magazine and acquired the ownership of it, had come to realise just how lethal the sport could be, even with his own safeguards in place. He turned the offer down flat, passing up a king's ransom. The man had a code of ethics not all that common in the higher reaches of the film industry.

With the weather now rapidly closing in across Europe, an offer of a more southerly exposure came with a call regarding a picture shooting in Naples, *The 'Human' Factor*.

I'd been there once before, hosting a USO show in the NATO

base that overlooked the wonders of Capri, Sorrento and the Bay of Naples. Naples I remembered as being a city of vibrant and continual movement, operating, it seemed, on some kind of ongoing centrifugal force. Cars and mopeds never stopped running and pedestrians never stopped dodging them. I remember wondering whether they realised what a gift they had in the astonishingly beautiful setting of the bay and if they ever slowed down long enough to really take a look at what was around them.

The film had quite a credit list. Director Edward Dmytryk, once blacklisted by the McCarthy Un-American Activities Committee for being a Communist 'sympathiser' and forced to continue his career under a string of aliases, was now working again under his own name. There was Barry Sullivan, with a film career that stretched back over some 50 pictures and who had partnered most of LA's leading ladies and then become the proud father-in-law of Jimmy Webb, composer of 'MacArthur Park'. Another main player was George Kennedy, known latterly for the *Naked Gun* pictures but at this time for *Cool Hand Luke*, *Airport*, *Earthquake* and many others.

Others involved in the production but not as visible, were an alleged 'bagman' from up-state New York, members of the Neapolitan and West Coast 'families', and street gangs of ten and twelve-year-olds who caused long delays by wandering into shot just as the director called 'action'. This was the other side of the Bay of Naples.

The bagman would drift in and out of the picture several times, hang around for a few days and then just as suddenly disappear. It was strongly rumoured that he was carrying thousands of dollars in undeclared cash to periodically top up the film's finances. The money, said to be the takings from a number of questionable stateside operations, was carried about in a medium-sized flight bag that never left the bagman's shoulder.

Next to appear on the scene were representatives of the old world and new world Mafia. It wasn't difficult to distinguish one from the other. The old Naples-based 'soldiers' came with camel-hair coats and hat brims over their eyebrows. There suddenly appeared to be whole ranks of George Raft lookalikes everywhere you looked. The LA-based newer breed sported snap-brim hats, knife-edged suits and shoes so highly polished they made you blink. For the most part, they seemed to be just keeping an eye on each other. The Naples bunch protecting their local interests, the younger brigade seeing that the shoulder bag didn't 'take a walk'. Both groups huddled off and on, maybe to discuss who was going to shoot who first.

Meanwhile, on another front, the meagre ranks of the film's security staff were being taxed by the daily appearance of young Naples street gangs, artful dodgers all of them, well schooled in the ways of sidewalk savvy. Every ploy that could be conjured from staging mock fist fights, knocking over lamp stands, or scratching some under-part of themselves just as the camera turned on, was staged openly and with very little let-up.

Inevitably they would have to be doled out lunch money and a few lira more to clear off – but only until the next day, when it would start all over again. So Naples, like any other metropolis, had its underside, but it's still the only place I can recall where a waiter chased me for over 100 yards to return my wallet, which I'd completely forgotten and left on his table.

Grazie and arriverderci, Naples.

★ ★ ★

There was an unexpected summons awaiting me on my return to London. It said to get out to the L&M Stage complex at Pinewood Studios to suit up for some interplanetary exploration on *Space: 1999*, the UK sci-fi series that would soon be enjoying a surprising but well-earned climb up the international ratings ladder. It was a welcome way to get going again on home ground. Trading lines with Nick Tate and Barry Morse would be an even choicer prospect.

The 'Space Brain' script was created by Chris Penfold and the director was the venerable Charles Crichton. My nameplate read 'Kelly – co-pilot'. I would take the seat next to Captain Carter (Nick Tate) on a mission to recover traces of an Eagle rocket craft, lost somewhere out in space. Co-ordinates reached, Kelly ventures out on a space walk for a closer inspection and is immediately engulfed in a white glutinous substance which disintegrates his brain (that's if I ever had one for taking this role) and transforms it into a conduit for a huge alien space brain. On return to Moonbase Alpha, a white-faced, demonic and gaunt-looking Kelly goes on the rampage until the space brain swamps the base with detergent foam. Exit Kelly!

More unfortunate still, however, was the final break-up of a partnership that had spread from a one-storey office studio in Slough to reach half way around the world. To say that what Gerry and Sylvia Anderson achieved was truly outstanding is an understatement. Breaking down international distribution barriers, fostering young home talent, producing a kind of entertainment that hadn't been formulated by anyone else – fresh, forward-looking and stylish, with standards they never allowed to dip. They brought a lot of happiness to many thousands of people.

But success is often a double-edged sword – it can be unexpectedly difficult to handle. The inevitable split that followed remains a private matter between Gerry and Sylvia. After the parting, each would follow the star of their own choosing and success would continue. But what most of us remember so well is that, during those first and continuing glory days, their partnership had placed them at the top table of total family entertainment.

Together, they were dynamite.

Chapter Eight

He has a brogue as thick and as soft as a pat of premium Irish butter. A voice that could run an octave within the space of a sentence and a span of anecdotes that could crease you in two or possibly endanger your health. Until recently he spent much of his time surrounded by columns and ledgers, running an accountancy firm overlooking Charing Cross Road. He has been adding and subtracting my career ins and outs for 40 years and has become a dear friend of Sheila and me.

His name is Frank Dunphy.

Figures, sums and economic realities I'm afraid I would leave solely in the hands of my wife, with one exception – my yearly and half-yearly fiscal visits to Frank, carrying into his office one elastic-bound packet of expense claims and another of earning statements. He would thank me for the bundles, give them a glance and then get down to the really important reason for our meeting, which was to stock me up on his latest crop of gags, behind the scenes intrigues and some of the wondrous happenings on London's West End stages.

He is now managing the career futures of Damien Hirst and other major artists in the arts and music fields around the world – they couldn't find a better ambassador. He enjoys people and it's very much a mutual arrangement.

★ ★ ★

Back in 1976, director Robert Aldrich had the picture, the perfect location and two of Hollywood's biggest stars, and then was absolutely stumped as to how he was going to use them. The picture was *Twilight's Last Gleaming*, the location was Munich and the two stars were Burt Lancaster and Richard Widmark. The problem was that, thanks to a long and bitter feud, these two couldn't even bring themselves to speak to each other, let alone be in the same room. All of which would make face-to-face dialogue very difficult – all right, impossible.

Aldrich came up with the perfect solution. The story concerned a renegade US military hero (Lancaster) who has commandeered an underground nuclear missile silo and is now threatening to 'nuke' Moscow as a protest against America's ongoing Vietnam War policy. Russia would automatically assume the strike was US-backed and all hell would break loose. Widmark, an establishment military officer based at ground level, is detailed to stop him. If that arrangement stayed in place, one of them underground, the other at surface level, the film could work. It did and powerfully well. In the movies, nothing is impossible.

That problem resolved, another was looming. David Healy and myself, cast as fellow officers under Widmark, were drinking coffee at a patio table outside the studio, surrounded by two-foot drifts of Austrian snowfall and wondering what we were going to do with our time off the next day. David was a warm and ebullient Texan who had served in England during World War II and stayed on to become one of the leading North American actors in Europe. He put down his cup, took another look at the nearest drift of snow and turned back to me.

'Did you ever go skiing?'

'Sure,' I answered. 'In Canada, up in the Laurentian mountains.'

'I made friends last time I was here with a couple who run a hotel in Kitsbuhl. Open invitation – want to go?'

Kitsbuhl was one of the 'in' winter resorts on the continent. It was a mouth-watering proposition.

'It sounds terrific. Are you sure we've got enough time?'

'It's usually only a couple of hours away and we're not on first thing the next morning, are we?'

'Okay, mein freund, you've got some company.'

We caught the early train next morning, were picked up by David's friends Helmut and Gerda at the station, and were on the 'piste' by 10.00am. What a time – a day filled with sun, crisp snow, a few spills and swift excitement. We had to take a taxi back to the station as Helmut and Gerda were busy with the hotel, making the train marked Munich with time to spare. Our spirits must have been flying from the exhilaration of the day, as neither of us noticed that the train, after more than an hour, was still climbing. But Munich, it finally occurred to us, definitely lay at a lower level. Then a look out of the window showed a chain of incredibly high mountains rising in the dusk ahead.

We had to face it, we were travelling in the wrong direction! But how? The front of the train had been clearly marked 'Munich' which always indicated the destination, didn't it? Well, no, not in Bavaria. We were informed by the conductor that the front sign on the train always designated where the train was coming from – we were in fact heading due north into the Swiss Alps! It was another 40 minutes to the next station, where we were told that there was no way we would be able to get back to Munich in time for our studio call the next day. Somewhat deflated, we each grabbed a frankfurter and a bench inside the station after confirming the time of the next Munich-bound train, wherever it was coming from.

Well, of course we were late and a quick rearranging of Aldrich's shooting schedule had been necessary. Whatever the Bavarian equivalent to 'being sent to Coventry' is, that's where we spent most of the day. But then things started to loosen up and David even risked a quip. 'Moscow still standing?' he asked. The response from the First Assistant was a slow smile, about one degree above lukewarm.

Next day, however, all was back to normal and we were once again in direct communication with Aldrich. He was known to get upset from time to time, but never to hold a grudge. He was that kind of man. Anyway, everything stayed in place above and below ground, the film went on to score both a critical and box-office success and Robert Aldrich gave a huge and genuine thank you to everyone who worked hard for it, including his two wandering Alpiners.

After this, I'd barely had time to change back into my 'streets' when a call came in to make an about-turn and skip over to Iver, the home village of Pinewood Studios. The usual security procedure demanded some proof of identification at the gate but, what with diving in and out of the place so often in those days, I guess my face was getting familiar enough to allow me entry with just a routine nod from the gatekeeper. Does wonders for the confidence, even though he could never be sure whether I was a member of the grounds staff or some eccentric hot-shot American producer. Everybody seemed to dress the same around there.

Except, that is, for John Dark, who was the producer I was calling on. When inside the Pinewood precinct, he was never without a shirt, tie and at least a sports jacket. John had attained, so it was said, a kind of legendary status at Pinewood as the longest-standing resident producer at the studio, although he never seemed to be behind his desk for more than five minutes at a time.

How he managed to parlay a picture-by-picture residency into something more or less permanent intrigued a lot of the Pinewood population. But it never went beyond that. I think the fact was, although utterly in awe of him, they also liked him. Usually when a picture had been shot and all the post-production finished, the producer and the production office would pull the blinds, hand in their keys and that would be that until the next outfit moved in. This apparently didn't apply to John Dark Esq. But then a lot of things didn't and, strangely, nobody ever appeared too bothered by it.

He came around from behind his desk, sporting a houndstooth-checked sports coat, with a crisp, white linen handkerchief tucked nattily into the top left pocket, and extended his hand, which I took.

'Seen you in a couple of things,' he began, 'and we thought you might do well with one of the roles in the picture.'

He gestured to the other figure in the room, who was leaning against the far side of the desk.

'This is Kevin Connor, he'll be directing.'

He was a youngish man, tall, lightly bearded, very handsome and dressed in a well-worn khaki safari jacket.

'Hi.' Kevin gave a slight nod and waved his hand in greeting.

John Dark in the meantime had returned to his desk.

'The role is the pilot Hogan. He's a freelancer, a bit of a maverick. That appeal to you?'

I barely had time to nod when he tossed two paper-clipped pages of script to me.

'Just take a brief look and we'll run a line or two.'

Sometimes you strike lucky – a line or two was all it took and I made my pilot's licence.

'We'll be leaving in two weeks' time for the Canary Islands, all right?'

'I'll be ready – thank you both.'

'It'll be nice having you along.'

John Dark didn't waste much time – his or anybody else's.

The company had produced a picture two years before titled *The Land That Time Forgot*, starring Doug McClure. McClure was the ideal lead, six feet of blonde, Malibu Beach good looks, a total charmer and as American as apple pie. The story had been left hanging with the disappearance of McClure and the forced departure of his friends. A mission 'back' had to be mounted to find out what had happened to him and so this year's follow-on adventure *The People That Time Forgot*. Leading the mission would be Patrick Wayne, second son of John, and very much bubbling in the mix were two ravishing beauties, Dana Gillespie and Sarah Douglas.

Sarah came along as a photographer-elegante to record the mission,

Dana was already there as a lusty tribal beauty who had fallen under the spell of McClure. The picture was, I suppose, stock fare in the cinematic adventure world, but Dark-Connor productions nearly always came with an unexpected edge and were sometimes referred to as hardcore Disneys – that was said tongue in cheek, but it was at least an attempt to distinguish them from Burbank's usual family frolics, which didn't stretch anybody over the age of seven.

McClure's star had risen with his featured appearances as Trampas in the top-rated Western series *The Virginian*. He became a kind of Pied Piper of La Palma, followed wherever he went by hordes of children chanting 'Trampas, Trampas'. And he never tried to escape them, only asked them quietly – as a favour to him – to calm down a bit before things got out of hand. That's all he had to do and there would follow a hush that would have been welcomed in any church – he was the magic man. He was also somewhat self-destructive, but spread a lot of joy on the way. I remember him with great affection.

La Palma is probably the smallest of the Canary Islands group, but outside the sprawl of the main town and out in its wild, unlived-in areas, in the great tracts of forest and soaring volcanic mountain reaches, it presents the timeless, untouched beauty of a world that has been left far behind. It was the ideal terrain for the story and, judging by the look of pleasure on John Dark's face, the perfect place to spend the next few months. And so to the story.

Hogan (yours truly), a freelance pilot with a twin-cockpit World War I aircraft for hire, has been contracted by the expedition party to take them back to the prehistoric island where McClure, a few months before, had been captured and imprisoned. They hope in some way or another to get him out of there. The adventure gets off to a shaky start when Hogan comes off second-best after some air-to-air combat with a giant pterodactyl and crash-lands himself and his party on a lava-covered mountainside. Nobody is injured, except the plane, which won't be flying again until the end of the picture. Leaving Hogan to engineer the needed repairs, the expedition party tracks back to where McClure had been captured and, after a hair-raising rescue operation through crocodile-infested lagoons, projectiles of flaming rocks and cannibal tribesmen, they get him back to the mountainside and the waiting Hogan and manage their escape.

We exited the island after an idyllic summer shoot, with Doug McClure announcing to all that John Dark's pictures just kept getting more and more enjoyable to work on and maybe there'd come a time when we would have to pay an entry fee to get in on them. An additional bonus was having Sheila fly over for a few days' break.

The island was a kind of time-capsule experience that we'd probably not all share again, our emotions were mixed on our coming re-entry into a civilisation we'd left some weeks before. For me it had been the most pleasurable location interlude I'd ever experienced – except, that is, for one nightmarish mid-morning confinement inside the small-sized lift of our Parador.

The lift mechanism chose the middle of a holiday weekend to grind to a halt with just me in it and the nearest service engineer a few hundred miles away on a two-day break in Morocco on Africa's north-west coast. Writer Tony Barwick could probably have written me out of this mess, but I certainly couldn't think of a way. Nothing worked inside the elevator, not even the alarm bell. There couldn't have been anyone else in the whole place, no one to hear my loud and repeated flails against the door.

I began preparing a list of who I was going to shoot first, once I escaped. When the list grew to include practically everyone we knew on the island, I decided to stop, call on some self-reliance, let go the panic and think a little more clearly. That directed my hand to my back pocket and a ring of keys, one of them the rather large key to my room. There was a six-inch wide reinforced glass panel at eye level in the centre of the lift door. I focused on it, wound up and whacked it with everything I had. I've never hit anything so hard in all my life – Ian Botham could hardly have matched it. A tiny crack appeared lengthwise in the glass.

Heartened, I drew back and walloped it again, this time breaking the surface, just as the manager appeared ashen-faced outside the door and yelling 'Madre de Dios, señor!' He was frozen to the spot, staring down at the splintered glass lying in a shambles across the floor and then back up to me still inside the bloody lift. I wasn't sure whether his concern was for his incarcerated guest or having to find some replacement glass. I'm still not.

★ ★ ★

My return from La Palma in the summer of 1976 was just in time for the final castings on *Star Wars* at Shepperton Studios, meaning that I managed to get an afternoon's interview with director George Lucas's friend Steven Spielberg on the last day, which in turn got me the last speaking part of any consequence in the film. I liked Spielberg; it would have been hard not to, he was completely down to earth during the meeting and gave you a generous-sized comfort zone.

Two weeks later I reported for duty as the Incom Engineer, a kind of head honcho of the ground crew, responsible for getting R2-D2 into his cockpit for the final campaign assault. It looked a cinch; in fact, it turned out to be anything but. We'd manage to squeeze one portion of R2-D2's body into place only to see some other part of him pop out for no apparent reason. R2-D2's plastic-plated structure had been shaped around the real 3'6" frame of one of filmdom's most-seen 'little people', Kenny Baker. On this particular sequence at Shepperton Studios, the operation went wildly out of synch.

It took over a day to get through all the permutations and finally get R2-D2 securely slotted inside, just as George Lucas ambled over to enquire what was holding up the attack preparations. This sort of thing could lose you a war.

Cubby Broccoli had no such problems, though there was little doubt that since the retirement of Sean Connery after *You Only Live*

Twice and his 1971 reprise in *Diamonds Are Forever* (both of which I appeared in), the fortunes of the Bond franchise had gone into a gradual decline. This despite the excellent choice of Roger Moore as the new Bond.

Roger was quite a tactician, though. Sean couldn't be outgunned on his own terms; his playing of the Bond character was 22 carat gold. So Moore had to come at the role from a different angle. Where Connery used brawn, Moore opted for finesse. Where Connery's eyes could hold a swift danger for those who risked a look, Moore's were a guileless sky blue until an acutely raised eyebrow turned them into lasers. Connery was always an enigma, it was a part of his strength. There was a shuttered side to him that the public couldn't get a look into. Moore came in through another door. His Bond was affable, charming and irresistible – and it worked.

Just how well it worked – after a couple of try-outs in *Live and Let Die* and *The Man with the Golden Gun* – I would get to see for myself during the shooting of *The Spy Who Loved Me*, the film that put the Bond pictures back on top.

I had been taken on board as Captain Carter of the nuclear submarine *USS Wayne* – a nice upgrade from my first two entries into the 007 ranks. The Wayne had been scaled down to about a third of the size of an operational sub, which still made it an awesome sight. But the 007 Sound Stage, which housed it, was even more colossal, at the time the largest ever built. Ken Adam had done it again.

Most of the crew and myself had served together before in a number of around the world combat zones, from the American Civil War to convoy duty in Korea to being part of the Allied invasion of Germany, all of them of course played to camera with hotel accommodation and lunch breaks thrown in, after which we would go out and batter the enemy (the ones who didn't speak very good English) absolutely senseless. So there was a great spirit of bonhomie around the under-deck of the *USS Wayne*, and a good thing too, as the close-quarters conditions made an elbow in the neck or a knee in the back almost inevitable. It was a little like travelling on a morning rush hour tube train – very close-quarters stuff.

Despite the Commander Bond insignia and that familiar film face, Roger moved among the crew as one of them, neither asking for nor expecting any kind of privileges, one of the boys. He had a way of bringing people and things together – there was little argument as to how popular he was with everybody.

Barbara Bach definitely aroused her share of attention, albeit of quite a different nature. She was a delightful lady and her shower scene in the captain's quarters drew people from every nook and cranny of the studio, some of whom probably hadn't seen each other for months. There hadn't been a gathering like it since the time of the last fire drill. The place was packed. It's a wonder no one thought of selling tickets.

The only downer in the shooting took place in the *USS Wayne*'s Control Room with the crew trapped under a heavy rocket attack. As usual, those of the crew who had fallen were told to hold their last positions until the order 'cut' was given. Ordinarily this would have caused no problem, but someone, not taking into account the relatively low height of the ceiling, had loaded the special effects gear with over-the-top explosives. When they were detonated in the limited height of the room, the ceiling paint was seared into white hot embers which then rained down on some of the prostrate members of the crew, who, still under orders, lay there waiting for the 'cut' signal to end the scene.

Roger and I had been crouched near the control door to make a hasty escape and did, without realising the effects of the explosion on some of the fallen members of our crew. The injuries were real and some painful, as was the enquiry that followed. The episode was an unfortunate rarity, despite the highly dynamic special effects now insisted upon by current filmmakers.

★ ★ ★

After getting shot at and nearly blown up in *The Spy Who Loved Me*, it was time for a family holiday. So we organised our vacation gear, most of it already secretly packed behind my back, loaded it and ourselves into our VW Camper and hit the road for our favourite holiday spot at Kidwelly. It was part of the Carmarthen area of Wales in a beautiful valley called Gwenllian, named after a dashing female warrior who had led her Cymru army in repelling waves of Norman invaders during the 12th century. We had been once before and had been longing to get back ever since.

Our destination was a cottage called Pennybach, built by the river on a huge acreage of rolling land owned and farmed by Howard Davies. It was ideal romping ground for the boys – well, for all of us – with sheep, cattle, fish and fowl in view everywhere and fresh salt breezes coming in from the sea just a mile away. Howard had a powerboat moored there and the trip we treasured most was down the coast to the bay at Laugharne, where Dylan Thomas had spent his time and the old white-painted garage, where he used to pen his magically musical poetry, was still there.

In the evening, and with the boys tucked away, Sheila and I would find a close-by hostelry and drink a toast or two to the day. It was no secret, certainly not to the constabulary, that most of the pubs in the town had what they called the 'backroom', which opened the moment the town curfew was rung and allowed drinking and singing to continue, sometimes till dawn was breaking over the hills. That male voice choral song was glorious.

On our last day and finally out for a family walk, we passed an old pub with a rather large coal heap out back, with what appeared to be a small, grey-coated animal tethered to it. On enquiry we were told that it was a puppy and, since it had no family and nobody could be found to take care of it, they were going to be forced to turn it loose and let it fend for itself. Now, what do you do on hearing a tale like this in the close company of your three young sons and a suddenly very quiet wife? Well, first of all, you wash it off to see what you've got under all that coal dust, which was a lovely reddish blonde coat with a face and nature that would have been impossible to abandon. We thanked the pub owners, bundled him into the back of the Camper with his three young new-found masters, named him Taffy and headed back home. Now we were six.

Chapter Nine

'Billion Dollar Bubble' was a highly intriguing TV drama documentary directed by Brian Gibson for the BBC's *Horizon* series. It went out in November 1976 and was a step-by-step account of probably the biggest insurance fraud ever perpetrated on the American public. Unbelievably, at the peak of their operations, the relevant company had issued more policies than there were people in the adult US population. That takes some doing. Each new sale would 'up' the value of the company and people were lining up to buy in.

At the head of the company and the 'operation' was Sam Wanamaker as the managing director, aided by a young and enthusiastic Hollywood newcomer, James Woods, whose dialogue delivery could out rattle a Sten gun. James and I were colleagues and fellow conspirators doing our best to keep up with the massive in-flow of premium payments on policies that were totally worthless. Something that had to be very carefully watched during the shoot was any instance of straying from the actual trial transcript, which would have instigated a case of misrepresentation for those sitting in the dock back in Chicago. Woods talked so fast and had me doing the same, I think a clanger or two might have been made, but we got away with it.

Luckily, I've had the good fortune of being co-opted into several BBC documentary productions over the years. The quality has never lessened, and it's always a delight to be in the line-up. To top it off, the canteen offered a consistently fine daily menu.

On my next TV call-up, however, I shifted channels and changed my old *Thunderbirds* togs for a NASA space suit worn by a slightly fictionalised American astronaut named Bob Grodin. This was for what Anglia TV claimed was the real story behind one of the first Apollo landings on the moon, a story withheld from the public. The TV film, *Alternative 3*, was directed by Christopher Miles from a documentary-style script by David Ambrose. Miles was the son of actor Bernard Miles and brother to actress Sarah. He and Ambrose had collaborated successfully on this kind of reportage before. The film played on contemporary rumours of a secret collaboration between Russia and America to establish an elite colony in space in the event of a catastrophe on earth, linking it to the unexplained kidnappings of a number of leading world scientists.

The Apollo crew were radio-linked to NASA through the American NBC network and their conversations transmitted to the public. However, there was speculation that another link line had been installed which was for NASA and government ears only. This line carried an excited report by an Apollo crew member 'named' Bob Grodin on what appeared to be an illuminated installation already present on the surface of the moon. Nobody aside from NASA and the government were ever allowed access to that rumoured report. After the return of the Apollo to earth, Grodin was reported to have developed a drink problem (the government version), and was later committed to a psychiatric hospital and rarely seen in public again.

The production was scheduled to air on 1 April 1977 – April Fool's Day, which might possibly have provided a hint to the factual content of the programme. But it was delayed by a technicians strike until 20 June. It was an intriguing concept, despite my having to hold ice cubes in my mouth to prevent Grodin's breath from showing in a cold March interview when the sequence was supposed to have taken place in mid-July. When *Alternative 3* was finally aired, the Anglia switchboard in Norwich was jammed for the best part of two days.

★ ★ ★

Flash forward to October 1977. The island of Malta, hardly more than a tiny sprawl on the blue-green shimmer of the Mediterranean below, had suddenly appeared out the port-side windows of our chartered aircraft.

'There it is – that's Malta!'

'Jeez, you think it's big enough to land this thing on?'

'I think they've probably looked into that.'

The voices came from the seats just behind me, the first belonging to John Ratzenberger, the second, with a noticeably heavy Brooklyn accent, was that of Hal Galili. Hal had come over to the UK with the original cast of *West Side Story*. A few years later, John Ratzenberger would sign on for a postal route on Boston's east side and spend his nights around a downtown bar called *Cheers*. Just now, both had been enlisted as crew members of a 19th century schooner that would be the sea-going base of operations for John Dark's latest voyage into the unknown.

This one, however, would be deep under the sea and not on it. Malta in its time had been alternately occupied by the Phoenicians, Greeks, Carthaginians and Romans, and in 1503 it became the home lodgings of the crusading Knights Hospitallers. One wondered how its chances of survival would rate with the invasion of John Dark's *Warlords of Atlantis* film unit.

The exploration had been mounted to discover evidence of the legendary and highly advanced island civilisation of Atlantis, said to have been devastated by a massive earthquake and then fallen to the bottom of the sea. Doug McClure was back as the co-leader of the expedition along with Peter (*The Onedin Line*) Gilmore, who'd sailed a few clippers in his salty career. As captain of the schooner I was in charge of organising the descent of the diving bell which would take us all to the sea bed. Of course, there turned out to be a surviving colony there, unfortunately full of criminal purpose, who immediately took us prisoner and slung us behind bars.

Our enemies were under the unlikely rule of Cyd Charisse, but hardly a protest was heard. With those long MGM legs she could have governed the universe. Some of the male contingent of the film crew were already rehearsing a few Gene Kelly dance steps, just in case.

In the meantime, Ratzenberger and Galili, who knew their way around a locked cell, freed us in time to make a harrowing escape to the surface. Harrowing for me especially because I'd been mistakenly given heavy brogues and trousers of sail cloth, triple the weight of what I should have been wearing in the water. On our swim back to the schooner and the camera, I began to sink and to thresh around wildly, which the film crew took to be part of the performance. In desperation, and sensing I could surface only one more time, I got my head above water and screamed out every expletive I could think of. Bert Hearn, the props master, was the only one aboard to twig what was going on. He dived overboard, grabbed me and hauled me back to the ship. Bert, I'll never forget you!

But my troubles weren't over. The film climaxed in a fearsome attack by an epic-sized octopus that seemed to have singled out the ship and captain for some special mayhem. The special effects team surpassed themselves. Not only were the tentacles the thickness of a grown man's girth, they were charged with an electric current and then coated with a slithery wallpaper paste that made them almost impossible to defend against. I'd rather have been in the ring with Mike Tyson. But it was my first outing as a genuine screen 'heavy' and, despite the narrow squeaks, a treasured screen memory.

★ ★ ★

In 1978, director Peter Hyams made a straightforward wartime romance starring Harrison Ford, Lesley-Anne Down and Christopher Plummer, titled *Hanover Street*. Ford was part of an American squadron based in England who seemed, judging from his 'chip on the shoulder' attitude, to be doing his best to lose the war for the

Allies. As Colonel Ronald Bart it was my thankless assignment not only to programme the missions, but to keep pilot Halloran (Ford) under control. He was a helluva dissenter to deal with – every briefing would produce a new confrontation. Harrison was so good at it, on a couple of occasions I really got irritated with him!

Anglia TV's London rehearsal rooms were situated just a stone's throw from the Chelsea Embankment, where run-throughs were scheduled to start on the latest instalment of the Roald Dahl series *Tales of the Unexpected.* The episodes had been a big hit for Anglia and they were hoping it was going to continue that way with the signing of one of the most flamboyant, and sometimes most infuriating, characters in the musical and revue worlds of both Britain and America. Her name was Elaine Stritch, the stage darling of Noël Coward and later Stephen Sondheim and films like *A Farewell to Arms* and Woody Allen's *Small Time Crooks.* The lady knew her way around. The director, Herbie Wise, had brought me in to play her husband in an episode titled 'My Lady Love, My Dove', a typical Dahl story of an attempted but botched con job by one neighbouring couple on another, with a surprise comeuppance at the end.

Two incidents linger in the memory about Elaine. As we were shooting a scene in the studio bedroom in preparation for the 'set up', I sat rather heavily on the dressing table chair, splintering it to pieces, landing myself in an undignified sprawl on the carpet.

As I scrambled awkwardly to my feet, Elaine shouted 'Don't get up! Stay there! Denis Norden could use it on *Alright on the Night!*' She was referring to a 'bloopers' compilation show, *It'll Be Alright on the Night*, that had started on British TV a few years before and would run for three decades.

My spine was locked, half way between coming up and going down, so I replied weakly, but with some venom, 'I'm sorry, my head was spinning, I couldn't think straight.'

'But all you had to do was just lie there.'

Sure. There I was with probably a twisted sacroiliac and she's concerned about a TV extract!

'Maybe,' I said through gritted teeth. 'I didn't want to spend the rest of the day flat on the floor.'

She chortled, actually chortled: 'You all right?'

She then put out her hand and helped me straighten up the rest of the way and we got on with the shoot.

A few days later, when our 14-year-old son Damian, who had recently developed diabetes, visited the studio and she heard about it, she took him aside for all of half an hour, had him talk about his diet, the difficulties he was having and how he was getting on with it. I glanced over a few times, you could see the effect she was having on him; the reassurance was showing all over his face. Elaine had been dealing with her own diabetes for a number of years.

So, when the time came the ebullient Miss Stritch was never slow in offering a hand in comfort.

Well, that was one tale of the unexpected. Another was just about to unfold in Paris in the shape of Peter Sellers' latest comic adventure. My involvement started with a phone call from my then agent, Steve Kennis of William Morris, one of the biggest film and theatrical managements.

'Just had an offer for you in a film shooting in Paris in four days' time,' he said. 'They want you to play J Edgar Hoover, the head of the FBI.'

'I really hate that guy!'

'Yes, he does seem to have alienated just about everybody. It may be a very helpful attitude to have in playing the part.'

'Are you going to tell me the name of the picture?'

'Yes, I guess I'd better – but I'm only going to say it once. They're calling it *The Fiendish Plot of Dr Fu Manchu*.'

'Mind saying that again?'

'Once is all you get. I'll send along a script and all the arrangements. By the way I'm going to be in Paris from Wednesday. I'll buy you dinner.'

Steve and I had got together after the *Rollerball* film premiere in London. He represented James Caan, and after the premiere I joined the club. Steve would probably have made a better than average actor – he definitely had a flair for the dramatic. So far the arrangement was working out very well, but you were never sure what was going to happen next. Meantime the *Fu Manchu* producers had come up with some high-octane acting talent in support of Sellers – each would be a plus. Sid Caesar, a cult comedian from the CBS Television network in America, Helen Mirren, John Le Mesurier (Sergeant Wilson from *Dad's Army*) and Stratford Johns of *Z Cars* fame.

Our hotel was perched at the edge of the Bois de Boulogne on the outskirts of Paris. I say perched, because viewed from the taxi in the descending dusk with its high, isolated Gothic outline, it bore an eerie resemblance to the horror motel in *Psycho*. Once inside the lobby, I half expected the spectre of Norman Bates to rise up from behind the reception counter and pass over the room key. At that precise moment, the lightbulb in a corner wall bracket chose to flicker – that about did it. I stayed just long enough to check in my luggage, tell the desk I wouldn't be using the shower, then quickly dialled Steve Kennis' hotel number.

'Hey,' he said. 'Are you ready?'

'Very,' I answered.

'Great – meet us upstairs in Maxim's at nine o'clock.'

'Okay. Who's us?' I asked.

'I'm bringing along Omar Sharif – don't be late!'

That's my agent – always with a joke! But over a contract, he was dead serious.

Fifteen minutes later, I was following the maître d' up the curving staircase to the first floor of Maxim's de Paris, one of the world's most celebrated restaurants. A softly lit central chandelier shone down on a dozen discreetly placed tables. The entire decor was done in a deep opulent red. At one of the tables along the wall sat Steve Kennis, across from him was Omar Sharif – one of William Morris's most treasured clients. The wine flowed and the conversation rolled on almost uninterruptedly for the next two hours. Omar was probably the most naturally courteous and engaging man I'd ever met. At 11 o'clock we regretfully called a halt to the talk and tippling. Paris studios, like the ones in Rome, didn't even think about filming until at least noon. The curfew time was just about acceptable.

Next day at 12.05 it was down to business. The late writer Sax Rohmer had parlayed his most sinister 'diabolique' character, Dr Fu Manchu, into a shelf full of books and films. He'd loved writing the macabre and in Peter Sellers he found a ready soul mate. Sid Caesar was probably one of the funniest men anywhere and on their first scenes together he had Sellers in continual hysterics. Then suddenly it wasn't like that any more, the laughter stopped – dead. Sellers seemed less and less in evidence. They rejigged my schedule to fit in two of my scenes over the next two days. I wasn't happy with a word of them. J Edgar Hoover's character completely escaped me – the duplicity of the man just wasn't coming across. It was probably the least satisfactory performance I'd ever come up with.

On the next day of the shoot, Sellers walked off the set to his dressing room looking ashen, saying he couldn't continue and needed a flight back to the heart clinic in Switzerland where he'd recently been receiving treatment. He would return to the film only with the okay of the specialist. We never saw him again.

What a career – what a loss. Goodbye Peter.

Chapter Ten

In 1979 Dick Lester had taken over from director Richard Donner on *Superman II* and came back later for the third. I managed to be signed on for both. The first was back in yet another space control room, tracking down an incoming destruct mission by a trio of villains from Superman's home planet of Krypton. I vowed then that if any more control room casting queries came in, I was going to charge a consultancy fee.

Three years later, the *Superman III* offer came with an upgraded flight to Calgary, Alberta and the role of a totally out of his depth Sheriff, attempting to cope with a raging oil refinery blaze and hundreds of the local population who'd come out to have a look-see. From my role as Chief Law Enforcer, I was able to catch an intriguing insight into the dollar power of a major Hollywood company. Calgary's high street was the main arterial route through town – the traffic was non-stop and heavy. The picture needed an unrestricted shooting area of the same size along with Calgary's big building backdrop for Superman's flying sequences. What did they do? Only detoured all the through-traffic around the town and leased the entire main street and everything around it for a week! The cost would probably have financed another moon landing.

Calgary was the oil capital of Canada and also the home of the upcoming Calgary Stampede, one of the most rousing, flamboyant rodeo round-ups in North America. The film company had guaranteed they'd put out the fire, take down all the high-flying wires and return the main street to the city before the Stetson bunch rolled in. They got it done just as the first covered wagon was about to enter the city. Job done, I pocketed my sheriff's badge, hopped a flight east and enjoyed two weeks with my sister Noreen and her husband Jack's family and many old friends in their huge rambling home in Toronto.

The '80s presented a goodly amount of possibilities, some realised, others not quite. Frederick Forsyth was back on the best-seller lists and almost immediately into a picture deal with *The Dogs of War*, a thriller about mercenaries conniving in a West African political take-over. Christopher Walken, an intriguing kind of actor who had managed to side-step the usual Hollywood route march since his *Deer Hunter* days, played a veteran officer who had gone through a number of freelance incursions and had now been recruited to head up another. I was Dr Oaks, a Harley Street consultant with white coat and heart monitor, hired to see if he was fit enough to handle it. At best his case looked borderline. He eyed me closely as I finished the examination.

'I know what you're thinking, but it's just to get me through one more time.'

'Maybe you've passed that point already.'

'One more, Doc, that's all. It's really important!'

So he got his conditional okay, which apparently satisfied his employers, and off he went to war. Me, I was shattered after having to learn paragraphs of medical techno-terminology by heart and then reel it off like a Dr Schweitzer.

Two quite different but linked events came into play a few months later in a Christopher Miles film tribute to writer D H Lawrence, titled *Priest of Love*. The first was my signing up for the picture. The second, and not quite so welcome, was the fact that, after a 500-mile flight down the US west coast to the film's location in Mexico, I contracted a virulent strain of intestinal disturbance, lightly referred to as Montezuma's Revenge.

The film starred Ian McKellen as Lawrence, Janet Suzman as his wife Frieda and Ava Gardner as the marvellously distracting Mabel Dodge. The events of the story actually took place in the state of New Mexico in the United States, a site which would have been of great relief to yours truly, as it would have ruled Montezuma out of the picture. My role was that of a US Immigration Chief who, forewarned of Lawrence's arrival in the state, was waiting to confront him with a subpoena in one hand and a copy of D H's *Lady Chatterley's Lover* in his rear pocket. However, the British Consulate interceded, Lawrence was allowed to stay and the Immigration Chief kept the book.

But the filming troubles had only started. The night before the final day's shooting, Montezuma's spell struck with a terrible vengeance. I couldn't move and could hardly speak, but the sequence had to be completed. They carted me to the location, brought in a camp bed and placed it just under the level of the camera lens. All I had to do was rise up from the bed, do the scene, hopefully in no more than one take, then sink back to the horizontal and out of sight. It took two takes but we got there. What a hero!

★ ★ ★

There's always a mighty good reason why the stars get to where they are. How Warren Beatty ever managed to secure multi-million dollar backing and then distribution for a film commemorating the life of the leader of the American Communist party, John Reed, remains one of Hollywood's longest running guessing games. Then, just to show he could work the other side of the street, he went on to direct, co-write and star in the film as well. It might have had something to do with the main players who rallied around Beatty to make *Reds* – Diane Keaton, Jack Nicholson, Maureen Stapleton, Gene Hackman and Paul Sorvino. And certainly with the all-seeing eye behind the camera, belonging to the young, virtuoso cinematographer Vittorio Storaro.

I had been called in to meet up with Warren Beatty a few days after his arrival in London. We seemed to have hit it off pretty well and a role in the picture looked a fair possibility. But then it was two weeks later and nothing had moved. It's one of the hardest things to do in this business, handling the waiting thing. You attend to other matters, keeping your focus on them as best you can, but the mind has a whim of iron that keeps flipping back to where you least want it to go. Even if it meant losing the picture, I wanted free of it. Just where I got the moxie for what happened next, I don't know, maybe from the extra glass of vintage claret at dinner.

I telephoned the *Reds* production office, explained who I was and was told that Mr Beatty wasn't there at the moment. He could be reached on his car phone, however, and they gave me the number. I could hardly believe this was all happening.

'Hello, Warren?'

'Yes, who's this?'

'Shane Rimmer – I was in to see you a couple of weeks ago and I was – '.

'Was that two weeks ago? Yeah, I remember, how are you?'

'Okay, but I was wondering what was happening. Pardon for being blunt about this, but if it doesn't look like I'm in the film, just tell me. Don't leave things hanging like you did in that porch scene with Faye Dunaway.' (What am I saying???)

'In *Bonnie and Clyde*? You didn't like that, huh?'

'Well, it was a pretty tough scene, but I didn't think it was really that convincing.'

'Shane, call me in the morning, okay?'

I hung up thinking I might as well have taken a cup of hemlock as made that call – but curiously enough I felt a lot better having done it. As best as I can recall, that's the way the conversation went with Warren Beatty.

I called production next morning and was told I'd be doing the part of MacAlpine, one of John Reed's oldest friends in the picture. Warren Beatty didn't leave that one hanging.

But it was up in Manchester, filming a party member's rally, where he pulled his master stroke. Due possibly to the amount of takes – sometimes over 50 – they'd had to sit through as members of the party, the extras were starting to look frayed and anything but enthusiastic. But the committee speeches droned on and on until a number of them were lurching forward in their seats, most of them on the brink of falling fast asleep – not really the type of response Beatty was looking for.

Then I noticed him huddled in a corner with Paul Sorvino, playing one of the leading committee members, each of them from time to time taking a look across at their yawning band of followers. Suddenly Sorvino wheeled away from the conversation, headed for the centre of the room, turned and pointed an accusing finger back at Beatty in an absolute rage. Beatty, his face flushed, almost ran at Sorvino, geared for a fight.

Suddenly the entire audience around the room sat up electrified, hanging on every word and gesture of the confrontation. Nobody seemed to notice the three cameras whirring away around the room, covering every row of the now transfixed assembly. Then, at the very point when each of them drew back their right hands for the pay-off punch, Beatty and Sorvino both stopped in their tracks, chuckled, then threw their arms around each other.

The fight had been beautifully staged and Beatty had got the wide-eyed crowd reactions he needed. Some man! Some director – Hollywood certainly thought so, saluting him with the Best Director Oscar for 1981.

★ ★ ★

Back in 1963 the Indian diplomat Matilal Kothar had attracted Richard Attenborough to the idea of making a film on the life of Mahatma Gandhi. Attenborough was intrigued, the studios were not, the project was turned down cold. But an Attenborough scorned can be a tough, persistent customer. It took him 20 years to turn it around. He signed up Ben Kingsley, probably the only man who could do justice to the title role. Other star names followed – John Gielgud, Trevor Howard, John Mills – and the backing was there. Attenborough pinpointed the locations and secured the talents of cinematographer Billy Williams to film them. The cameras started to roll in November 1980 and a classic was born.

So, with not even a hint of a Raj accent or any Urdu-speak, how did I fit into all this? In a country of nationally known broadcasters and communicators, the National Broadcasting Company's Edward R Murrow was the most revered of them all. His wartime reportage back to America from the heart of the London Blitz in World War II probably swayed his millions of listeners into finally backing US entry into the war. Murrow, over the years, had become a close friend of Gandhi and had been deeply sorrowed by Gandhi's assassination. The family made a request that he report the full funeral proceedings in Delhi to the western world. I was given the Murrow role in *Gandhi* and was to fly out to India in three weeks' time to be filmed in a recreation of the procession.

Sheila had toured the main Indian hotel circuit some years previously with her dance act The Three Martinis and, under very strict chaperoning, had met many of the royal and near-royal luminaries on the Indian social scene. They would come into Bombay, Calcutta and Delhi on occasion to let down their hair and enjoy western-style weekends. Through some of these acquaintances, I suddenly had a full appointment list of maharajahs, princes and government officials to meet up with and I could hardly wait. Neither could a totally unexpected monsoon. It struck with calamitous force, wiping out sets and location set-ups and whatever was left of the next two weeks' filming schedule.

A quick revamp had to be organised. So I exchanged palaces, Kashmir princes, marble halls and government ministers for a small commentator's desk at Shepperton Studios, where I spoke the commentary while sitting in front of a back-projection showing Gandhi's funeral procession. But just seeing and speaking of that thousands-strong procession of mourners, even from afar, was intensely moving.

★ ★ ★

About the only connection I'd had with British theatre since coming to London was from the stall seats; I was a more experienced audience member than player. But things were about to change. Director John Schlesinger came a-knocking. He had been brought up in the theatre, both dramatic and operatic, but then converted to the cinema, directing *Billy Liar* in 1963 and hitting the jackpot in 1969 with *Midnight Cowboy*. He not only directed the picture with Dustin Hoffman and Jon Voight but dropped in a substantial amount of backing money. Helped by a load of pre-publicity, a lot of it on its controversial content, the film went on to become a smash hit and his investment return soared into multiples.

In 1981 he rolled the dice again, persuading the National Theatre to acquire the rights to a very earthy piece of Americana, Sam Shepard's *True West*. The story tells of the clash between two feuding brothers, played out in their family home on the outskirts of Los Angeles. Schlesinger cast Anthony Sher and Bob Hoskins as the brothers, banking on each to ignite the other's performance on stage. They went even further. On some occasions he must have been ready to put in a four alarm fire call.

Sher and Hoskins were electric. Patricia Hayes was their once resilient mother, now helplessly caught in the vortex whipped up by the two brothers. I played a rainbow-shirted Hollywood producer, determined to gain the rights to a promising screenplay by Hoskins, while attempting not to be totally derailed by the two-man blitzkrieg going on all around me. Schlesinger said to me once, 'If you ever find yourself caught between Sher and Hoskins, especially front stage, just remember to keep your feet anchored to the floor!' I did, but bucking the gale force of those two out there sometimes left you breathless, but always invigorated.

The writing of *True West* was stunning, filled with honest to God home truths. It played to a capacity house every time out and the only other thing that approached the pleasure of it was walking across Waterloo Bridge at dusk, with the whole of that night's South Bank entertainment lighting up the other side.

All that and a piece of off-stage family drama as well.

Sheila and the three boys had come along to the opening night party and the Green Room was packed with just about everybody who'd had a hand in the production. We suddenly realised after half an hour that none of our three sons was among them. Enquiries revealed that no one recalled seeing them during the last 20 minutes. Now ... where?

With three different theatres making up the National complex, there is a lot of interlinking going on in the areas backstage. It's not difficult to get totally lost just trying to locate the theatre where you're performing in time for your entrance. Newcomers were known to unwind a spool of twine as they ventured out in order to follow it back to where they started out. But this was worrying, all of the boys knew their way around the National, so why their absence? A search was quickly organised down every passageway and corridor but no trace of them could be found. The River Police were alerted and a general alarm was about to be sounded when Ben, son number two, appeared at the Green Room entrance looking absolutely ashen. I hurried over to him through the crowd.

'Are you all right? Where are the other two?'

He pointed back and upward. 'They're up in the air!'

'What are you talking about?'

'They're up in the air and I can't get them down.'

Tears began flooding his eyes.

'Where?'

'You won't be mad?'

'Of course not. Show me!'

He nodded and turned out of the entrance with half a dozen of us following. He led us straight to the backstage area of the Cottesloe Theatre. The place was strewn with sections of set, tables of props and one lone yellow forklift truck. The extension was up and sitting there a little rigidly, some ten feet in the air, were his two brothers. I shouted 'Don't move either of you. We'll get you down!'

As a matter of fact, they didn't look all that worried about the situation despite the anxious ring of faces looking up at them. Fortunately Frank, our stage manager, knew exactly how the truck operated and in a minute the extension was lowered and the two of them hopped back to ground level. At first I was going to let go a blast at all of them, then realised that despite playing it cool they were all pretty shaken up at what had happened. I let it go.

'Anybody want a coke?'

One afternoon after a matinée show near the end of the run, Bob Hoskins came over to me. 'Somebody wants to see you,' he said.

'What – who?'

'Hey, would I steer you wrong?'

He said all this in an almost perfect Bronx accent. He had about the best American sound over here. I should have picked up the hint. He crooked his finger without further explanation and I followed him up the stairs to the next floor. There was a rehearsal room in the corner, from which I could hear a piano being played and someone singing a very familiar Broadway song. He opened the door, where several people in workout togs were gathered around a piano. One of them was the young director Antonia Bird, who I knew but distantly.

'Hi Shane, thanks for coming in.'

'It's a pleasure. What's happening?'

As Bob turned back to the door, he nudged me gently on the arm. 'Sing pretty.'

He had walked me right into a try out for *Guys and Dolls*. So, what do you do?

I moved in towards the piano.

'Have you got some music?'

Antonia moved over and made room for me.

'Sit down and have a look at the score.'

I think I sang 'Luck Be a Lady Tonight' – and amazingly the lady delivered!

In the space of eight musical bars I became a member of New York's finest in the person of Lieutenant Brannigan, who would spend most of the play hot-footing it around Broadway and 49th Street, trying to catch up with the changing nightly venue of the city's biggest floating crap game. There was so much talent bursting out in that show, it would be hard to exclude any of them from mention, but to this day the performances of Imelda Staunton and Trevor Peacock remain stand-outs. And all this to the score of about the most exuberant, exhilarating Broadway musical ever created.

The finale was a stage-wide, up-tempo, full ensemble tap-dance number. Try as I might I just couldn't get my feet to find the rhythm. For me the chorus line was not a happy place to be. In desperation, but secretly to my deep relief, the company 'smithy' removed the taps from my shoes before everybody was driven crazy. I was dancing 'mute'. The last direction I had was 'Keep waving your hands and the audience won't take a look at your feet.'

One evening towards the end of the London run, the company was asked to stay on for a short time to meet up with a special guest who had expressed a wish to say thank you to the cast. Speculation soared as we waited on stage as to who it might be. Nobody came close. After a wait of just less than ten minutes, two rather elderly and beautifully tailored gentlemen entered from stage left followed almost immediately by the blue-gowned figure of the Queen Mother. She looked dazzling as she proceeded across the stage towards us but you could sense many of us wondering how she would take to being introduced to a gang of Lower East Side characters with such monikers as Benny Southstreet, Harry the Horse, Angie the Ox, Liver Lips Louie, Rusty Charlie and Big Julie.

The Royal lady looked a little apprehensive, I thought, but faced it quite bravely, as did her elderly entourage of six, who, after an initial stiffness, relaxed openly and greeted everyone in a very outgoing, warm-hearted way. It was a night, oh what a night it was – it really was.

One of the most revealing glimpses of how the craft of the theatre can be passed on to young hopefuls could be had from the window of our dressing room, which looked across the quadrangle to the dressing room belonging to Ralph Richardson, one of the most masterful actors of the British stage. Before his every evening performance in the Lyttleton Theatre, the younger and more recently enlisted actors would gather there in groups of twos and threes, some sitting on the floor, others leaning up against the wall, some asking questions, others just listening to that voice that never struck a false note. I was reluctant to ask any of them what in particular was exchanged on those evenings; best, I thought, if it was remembered just between themselves.

The National Theatre provided for the seasoned actors a playing field not always available in the commercial houses. And for that, every player who has walked those boards carries a special sense of gratitude. For the young, it could sometimes smack of a kind of gladiatorial training. But the rewards could be substantial and many fine actors still strutting their stuff across the world's stages can attest to that.

Chapter Eleven

There are some books which bring on a relaxed feeling every time you open them up. For me there is a row of nine on my shelves that rarely go undisturbed long enough to gather so much as a mote of dust. They were written by an American-born, London public school-educated, cantankerous, crusty and just plain masterly detective author who wrote like an angel, Raymond Chandler.

His unofficial precinct was called Bay City, but in reality he was writing about Los Angeles and the private eye who walked its 'mean streets' was Philip Marlowe. He stayed at the top both as novelist and Hollywood scriptwriter until his death in 1959. I was hooked on his writing ever since picking up a copy of *The Big Sleep*, his first Philip Marlowe novel, while browsing through a Charing Cross bookshop and I've been hanging on his every word (and chapter) ever since.

Powers Boothe, who had jumped up the Hollywood ladder with his dog soldier portrayal in *Southern Comfort* and then lost his place by ignoring a Hollywood actor's lock-out, had been brought over to play the TV lead in *Philip Marlowe, Private Eye*. It was a good choice. He had a laconic, wise-talking style that suited the Marlowe character perfectly. I was hired as Detective Lieutenant Del Murphy who, in the episode 'Smart Aleck Kill', was brought in to investigate a murder in which Marlowe appeared to be heavily implicated. It could have been a good match-up, but the script called on me to be beaten to the punch at every turn in the investigation, while Marlowe-Boothe sailed through, picking up clues as if he was on a paper chase, and handily nailed the killer. I'm not sure whether the lieutenant was able to hold onto his pension after that episode or not.

Fortunately, we were both chronic golfing nuts, so any rifts that arose in our scripted characters were ironed out from tee to green at the Richmond Golf Club. It turned out close enough for each of us to buy the other a pint of Best bitter. A nice round, Powers ... just!

★ ★ ★

Time for a family vacation – Sheila and I and our three teenage sons, Damian, Ben and Paul – but where? Then right on cue came an invitation from Pierre Luthi, a Swiss student who had stayed with us years before while on an English language course in London. The invitation was to visit him and his family in Rohrbach, just outside the city of Berne. It looked like the ideal solution. We arranged for a quick check-over for our veteran VW Camper from an auto mechanic friend, Frank. The 'quick' check over took five hours until 2.00am on the morning of our departure.

'You think it'll be okay?' I asked him.

'I think so, if you don't go over 80 mph up some of those hills.'

'That's a joke, right?' I said.

'Probably – how many miles have you got on her?'

'I don't know – the speedometer stopped at 200,000.'

'Just be sure your car insurance is right up to date, okay? Happy landings.'

And with that heartening exchange we motored off for the white cliffs of Dover as dawn was breaking.

The one reservation that kept niggling away at me was whether our Camper van could really manage to stay together for a run at some of the most awesome uphill and downhill travelling in the Alps. To skirt the most precipitous climbs we plotted a route over the gentlest looking ground we could find, which meant crossing the borders of France, Belgium, Holland, Germany and Luxembourg –

Luxembourg only because of an indecipherable German road sign which led us onto a newly opened autobahn going completely the wrong way and which we couldn't turn off for nearly three-quarters of an hour. That done, and after a brief stop in a layby to calm our 'angst', we continued in what we hoped was the right direction.

Although the engine had seemed to be turning over with only a few misses here and there, with every further kilometre the noise from the rear housing seemed to be amplified by tens of decibels. We could have been mistaken for a Panzer Division gearing down some of those hills. On our approach, now peppered by frequent explosions from the back end, sheep scattered, cows bolted and everywhere birds were taking off and heading for the clouds. Climbs of over 15 degrees were now very much in doubt – those approaching 40 degrees and up were definitely out. 'Frank – where are you?' we thought.

And so we chugged across our final border and into Switzerland and the now mandatory currency exchange to take care of such absolute touring necessities as triple-flavoured ice cream cones, a visit to an adjoining reptile house and a raft of comic books written entirely in German which the kids couldn't possibly understand – but they were knocked out by the illustrations.

After filling up the petrol tank, we decided it was time to check the storage space under the back seat holding our blankets, pillows and other teenage paraphernalia. What I saw, aside from the totally soaked condition of everything inside, was the asphalt surface of the road where the floor should have been. The hole was as big as a mine entrance and was the reason our engine had been amplifying to such an increasingly thunderous noise over the last 100 miles.

Fortunately, we were now just one hop away from our destination, where we hoped we'd be able to hang out the bedding and see if we could maybe acquire a sheet of armour-plating for the floor of the van. We turned into the only garage in Rohrbach for an inspection. The mechanic, however, declined to ramp up the sides for fear the engine would drop free of the chassis and crash down onto his floor.

So for the duration of the holiday, we parked it discreetly behind Pierre's grand family house, well out of sight of the village onlookers.

Rohrbach was great fun – the Swiss adore a young family and the lads got into everything from climbing 20 feet up the Eiger (the way they carried on about it, you'd have thought they'd set a world record), attending a pig roast on the spit at a neighbour's barbecue, and then visiting a colony of brown bears at the Berne Zoo, where one of them, taking exception to Damian on the other side of the bars, deliberately peed all over his shins. Now it was his turn to dry out on the line. But it had been a great journey and full of surprises, with most everything going like clockwork, which is how things are supposed to in Switzerland.

Miraculously, there were no further incidents on the trip back until the van groaned to a dead stop just 100 yards short of the ramp that led to our returning channel ferry – and with only a minute and a half to get aboard. Luckily, we'd come to a halt on one of the few level stretches of road we'd encountered on the whole trip. Leaving Sheila in the driver's seat, and hoping she wouldn't miss the ramp and plunge into the sea, the rest of us jumped out, bent our shoulders to the rear of the vehicle and got it aboard with just seconds to spare. What would happen at the other end, we didn't know, but after all the ups and downs on this side, it would be a piece of cake. Ha! On our return home, we awarded our venerable VW van a very honourable discharge and retired it to a breaker's yard.

★ ★ ★

Travelling to someplace new, possibly intriguing and certainly unknown, adds a particular buzz to any trip. But in 1984, after a ten-hour flight from London, the buzz was becoming a drone and my feet were itching for some contact other than the aisle carpet. Revival was at hand as the wheels of the aircraft touched down on the runway tarmac and rolled towards the white-washed, flower-decked approaches of Nairobi Airport. The passengers gave a relieved round of applause to the flight deck for riding most of the bumps and to the cabin crew for keeping us nicely fed and watered throughout. I was travelling in the company of three fellow actors who like myself had been signed up for a film that was scheduled to keep us sweltering under an African sun for the next six weeks.

John Rhys-Davies from *Raiders of the Lost Ark* and the Welsh valleys was in the seat ahead. Connie Booth, who had ironed out the awful blunders of her husband (and co-writer) John Cleese in *Fawlty Towers*, and John Savage, the young loner from *The Deer Hunter*, were belted alongside. We were all part of an American-funded adventure production called *Nairobi Affair,* and for all four of us it would be our introduction to Kenya and Charlton Heston, a sizable lot to handle in the first two days.

In the event, Heston was out game hunting with his son near Kilimanjaro and wouldn't be around until he carried back a trophy. After a recuperative night's sleep in Nairobi, the four of us boarded a medium-sized, twin-engined passenger plane headed for our base camp at the Masai Mara. There was little tedium on this one. Once you gained entry to the plane from a squat step-ladder at the rear, you walked up an incline into the main passenger area. I can't remember whether any seat belts went with the trip or not. But as the aircraft juddered upward to its cruise altitude, it brought to mind that grainy end-of-picture flight that took Ingrid Bergman away from Humphrey Bogart in *Casablanca.*

Nairobi had been the ideal entry to Kenya, colourful, welcoming, its markets teeming with every kind of fruit, vegetable and African handcraft. Now, from a height of 1,000 feet, we watched the approach of the Masai Mara escarpment, following the river all the way to Tanzania and our safari camp. After the bustle and ado of Nairobi, it looked almost aloof and as old as the world, giving little hint of the dark history of Mau Mau atrocities committed there back in the 1950s.

As our aircraft dipped into its descent path, the increasing noise of the engine alerted grazing packs of zebra, wildebeests and gazelles, who suddenly peeled off in every direction. It was an amazing, almost primeval sight. Then the wheels were back on level ground and we were on the incline again.

The one precaution advised after landing was to tread carefully on exiting – a mis-step down the aisle could propel you towards the rear exit in a very undignified heap. But that ceased to be our main worry when we glanced over to the river just 50 yards away and saw a family of hippos, half way in or half way out of the water, whichever way you chose to look at it. This was unsettling in that one of the cardinal rules of the African bush is to always give hippos and their young the widest possible berth. In any case, they appeared far too busy enjoying their bask in the sun to pay us much notice. Minutes later came the welcome sound of an approaching mini-bus pulling up in a cloud of dust to take us to the safari camp and the director, Marvin Chomsky.

Charlton Heston returned to the camp that evening carrying a rifle but not as yet a big game trophy. He joined the company at the head of the long communal dining table and proved an engaging companion, if sometimes a little heavy on right-wing rhetoric. But his recounting of various career anecdotes, from the noirish *Ruby Gentry* to an Orson Welles match-up in *Touch of Evil* and holding on for dear life during the chariot race in *Ben-Hur*, was matchless. A good evening's overture to the shoot.

'Okay everybody,' rang out the voice of the First Assistant, 'time to get to our pillows – first call, 6.30 in the morning!'

Still half numb from the day's scurrying about and with Charlton in the lead, although he appeared to have little idea where we were bound, we ambled out into the Kenyan dusk. Our tents were pitched separately on deep-cemented bases in a nearby semi-circle, each with a complete en suite arrangement inside, which made night-time trekking for ablutions unnecessary.

Happily, a great company spirit prevailed throughout most of the filming and – aside from a dawn-breaking trumpet reveille, sounded by an out of tune, over-zealous LA hand to mark the occasion of July the 4th, American Independence Day – all was peaches and tinned cream. But there were so many more compelling sounds reverberating through the dense surrounds of the camp, both day and night. The evening chatter of the bush babies, the scolding of mother baboons and the answering back of their young, the occasional deep-throated growl from the darkness just the other side of the river, and then the glorious day-long exuberance of the bird song. At one point, John Rhys-Davies turned to Connie Booth, nudged her and said, 'You know, this place is wilder than bloody Wales!'

★ ★ ★

Twenty-five years after making *Heaven Knows, Mr Allison*, Robert Mitchum and Deborah Kerr got together again under director Herbie Wise to film a nostalgic comedy, *Reunion at Fairborough*, in which former American GI Mitchum returns to where he had been posted during the war to tie up a few loose ends. This, for the purposes of filming, was the idyllic village of Shere in Surrey.

There is a certain aura that gathers naturally around a legendary front-line actor like Mitchum. No studio hype can fabricate it, not even the star himself can do much about it once the process starts. When he moves, everybody watches; when he speaks, they listen. The local villagers, let alone the cast, were entranced by him. And yet it was possibly as much a burden on him as it was a boon. Many performers have to work hard to project their characters. Mitchum, on the other hand, maybe had to work just as hard at reducing his.

He and Deborah Kerr were absolute magic together, much to the delight of old-timers Red Buttons and Barry Morse. But it was my character, Joe Szyluk, who, during a couple of heart to heart conversations to open up Mitchum's past, got out of him the revelation that he not only fathered Deborah Kerr's child but was now a grandfather as well. He was without doubt one of the easiest actors I ever worked with. Underneath what could have been misjudged as an everyday Hollywood veneer, he would engage you with such candidness it never cost an ounce of effort to go along with it and respond every bit as fully. You'd know if you hadn't!

I had met Mitchum once before at a crowded Richard Harris house party. There were a few held breaths when the two of them got together near the drinks cabinet, but they were obviously soul mates, and the only glasses raised were in toasts to each other and the room. A good thing, because either one of them could have been a total wrecking crew all on his own. Mitchum had only one altercation in the film that I was aware of and that was in protecting someone else from a rather heavy-handed assistant. It was one punch I think, but I heard later the assistant was sitting up and taking nourishment, albeit through a straw and thinking seriously about trying another profession.

So back from leafy Surrey and into the comforts of home. Out of a number of calls that week, two were of particular interest. The first was from Tony Barwick to say he was half way through the writing of a 'stop-motion' animated series about a Mr Magoo-type private eye; it looked like loads of fun and how about doing the voice? The invitation was a mouth-watering one. Tony, when the situation allowed, could write with a mischievous, off-the-wall brand of humour. The name of the gumshoe character was *Dick Spanner*. I had just about enough time to say 'Count me in!' when another call came in, this one from Denmark. Could I get to Copenhagen in three days' time? The cast list and script would be on the way.

Tommy Steele had a bit hit back in the 1970s with a song called 'Wonderful Copenhagen'. Well, it would be if only you could see it after three o'clock on a winter afternoon. We made it by 2.30, with just enough light left to glimpse what the singing was all about – it did indeed look 'wonderful'. But inside another 60 minutes the daily

Keeping an eye on Mark Hamill in *Star Wars*.

Waiting for the next assault in
The Spy Who Loved Me.

With Roger Moore in *The Spy Who Loved Me* – ready when you are, James.

Making *Warlords of Atlantis* with director Kevin Connor. 'It's okay, he's friendly.'

Like hell he is!

Arabian Adventure – it sure was.

In *Gandhi*, as Edward R Murrow commentating on Gandhi's funeral.

Meeting a real Canadian Mountie during the making of *Superman III*.

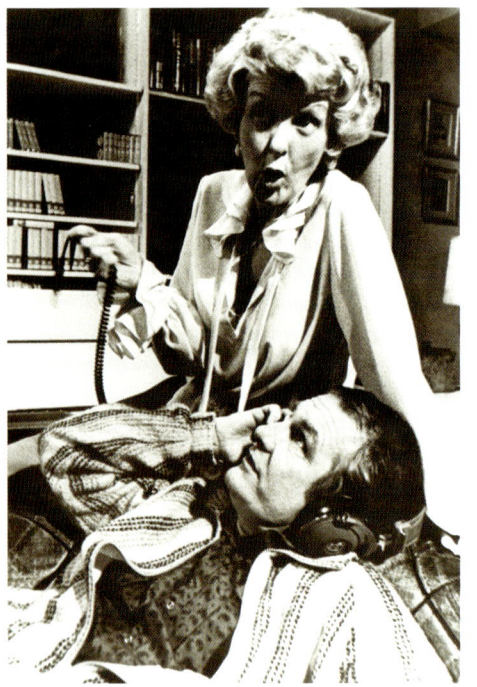

Playing games with Elaine Stritch
in *Tales of the Unexpected*.

As the plantation manager Belnap in *Out of Africa*.

On the coffee plantation with Meryl Streep in *Out of Africa*.

Private detective Dick Spanner props up the bar in the Big Pear.

My *Coronation Street* comeback.

★★
DAILY MIRROR, Friday, July 29, 1988   PAGE 15

Phantom of the soap opera returns to haunt show

STREET STAR SHANE'S BACK FROM THE DEAD!

By REGINALD WHITE

THE ghost of a murderer has come back to haunt Coronation Street scriptwriters.

The soap's writers brought in actor Shane Rimmer on Wednesday to play store boss Malcolm Reid.

But they had not reckoned with eagle-eyed viewers who spotted that Shane had already been killed off in a Street episode 20 years ago ... as a different character.

Loyal fans, worried about a Dallas-style back-from-the-dead farce, phoned Granada TV.

A Street worker said: "They were hoping nobody would notice."

But yesterday embarrassed TV bosses admitted they had been caught out by loyal fans.

TAKE ONE: Back in 1968 Shane played Joe Donelli, an old army buddy of Elsie Tanner's second husband Steve.

When American GI Steve was found dead after a brawl, Len Fairclough was suspected of his murder.

Dark

But it was Shane's character Joe who eventually owned up to the killing and shot himself dead after taking poor old Minnie Caldwell hostage at gunpoint.

TAKE TWO: Now Shane has turned up as Malcolm Reid — who has his own dark past.

Rovers barmaid Gloria identified him as the man photographed at Niagara

PAST: Shane with Elsie Tanner.

EXCLUSIVE

Falls with his arm around Audrey Roberts.

But she still does not know he is the father of Audrey's love child, Stephen.

A Granada spokesman said yesterday: "The fact that Shane is remembered from so long ago proves the loyalty and long memory of our large audience.

"But Shane is a very fine actor. He was the best man for the job and fitted the character of Malcolm Reid perfectly.

"We are very pleased to have him back."

PRESENT: Actor Shane (right) with Audrey and her watchful hubby Alf

Brits hit by a pong

THOUSANDS of British tourists may be evacuated from Venice ... because of a poisonous pong. Freak temperatures have clogged up the polluted canals with dead fish and mayor Antonio Casellati said yesterday: "It is a definite health risk and I may have no choice but to evacuate the worst areas."

With US professional golfer Johnny Miller, Tony Barwick and Barry Authors.

With Damian, Paul and Ben on Paul's wedding day.

On the mean streets of Zar XL5 in *Space Police*.   *Space Truckers* – you can't be serious...

Lipstick On Your Collar, with the up-and-coming Ewan McGregor (front).

Here's looking at you, Scott.

The family – (left to right) Jacky, Damian, Paul, Sheila, Kit, Catherine, me, Hugo, Ella and Ben.

winter quota of sunshine would be used up and we'd be fitting infra-red lenses to see the next three feet in front of us.

The cast list of *White Nights* was an intriguing one. The two headliners were both standout dancers, one classical, the other a hoofer, but neither had strayed too far into acting territory. That experience came from a trio of feature-playing ladies, Helen Mirren, Geraldine Page and Isabella Rossellini. A lot of scripts over the years have been based on the premise that the impossible is often more possible than you might imagine. Some of them never get to prove the point, others do. In *White Nights* a defecting Soviet ballet dancer crash-lands inside the Russian border, and is then helped in completing his escape by an American expatriate.

Far-fetched? Maybe, but it didn't really matter. In Mikhail Baryshnikov's playing of the Russian dancer, director Taylor Hackford uncovered a strikingly natural acting talent. In the dancer Gregory Hines, he found another, getting a toe-tapping, street smart performance in the role of the expatriate who rediscovers a lost allegiance to his country. What really matters during the course of the story is the almost hypnotic quality of the dance sequences, with each dancer following the other in his own style – one off the New York pavements, the other from the raked stage of the Bolshoi Theatre; they leave you absolutely breathless. I was lucky enough to watch them mapping out some of the core routines, but a lot of it was being left to moment to moment improvisation.

They put down such scintillating, inspiring footage I almost forgot what I was in Copenhagen for, which was to play the frazzled American ambassador Carlton Smith, who suddenly finds himself, because of the delicate circumstances of the defection, completely out of his depth. He ends up sandwiched between Soviet officialdom and the gung-ho directives of an American hard-right lady representative, played to the hilt by Geraldine Page. I got through it pretty well okay, but carried around some deep rib damage from the hefty elbow digs sent my way by the always enthusiastic Miss Page.

The location, of course, purported to be a rather gloomy and snow-banked Moscow, but there's enough going in this picture to light up any screen you might wish to view it on, and there'll be no border guards to duck.

★ ★ ★

Director Sydney Pollack, meanwhile, had corralled a trio of stars for a grand-scale panoramic film, *Out of Africa*, on the extraordinary life of Danish writer and Kenyan land-holder Karen Blixen. And he wanted to film it in and around the heartland of Kenya, where she lived and came to fame in the 1940s. Meryl Streep, with her linguistic flair, was the obvious choice for Blixen; Klaus Maria Brandauer was in as her husband, the blue-blood Baron, and as the adventuring love of her life there was Robert Redford. I was hired as the rather tight-lipped and taciturn American manager of the plantation, Belknap. Since little opportunity came up for conversation with the headliners, because of the sheer spread of the picture, I think I might have caught the taciturn part of his character with fair conviction.

The scenes taking place on Blixen's former coffee-producing farmland were filmed on the present owner's plantation. This was the wife of the former President of the Kenya African Union, Jomo Kenyatta. As well as that particular term in office, he spent seven years behind bars for an alleged involvement in the Mau Mau uprisings of the 1950s. The plantation, though, was an immensely impressive sight, financed (along with her husband's political career, it was rumoured) by Mrs Kenyatta's leading role in the country's most widespread and profitable 'black market' operation. That aside, the plantation was the ideal location in which to film the Blixen sequences, but for one production error.

A pivotal scene in the script called for row upon row of white flowering coffee bushes, just waiting to be harvested. Possibly the scheduling team had made a rare miscalculation in time zones, because by the time the camera unit arrived to film the blossoms, they had either withered or just dropped off. The sequence, as important as it was, looked out of the question. But a touch of on-the-spot resourcefulness changed the impossible into the attainable. A Kenya-wide search was mounted for all available stocks of shaving cream aerosols wherever they could be found. The cans came in by the truckload and were then sprayed up and down the rows of threadbare coffee plants, transforming them into a rich and bountiful looking, ready to pick harvest. Inspirational!

I found Brandauer a compelling talent. I had first seen him in the 1981 German film *Mephisto*, a resetting of the Faust legend, and in it he was spellbinding – he still is. Now he was in with two mega-star talents in Redford and Streep. But to many onlookers, including myself, his performance was the one you couldn't take your eyes from.

I was back and forth twice more during the course of *Out of Africa* – I had a ticket for Sheila to join me for ten days, but Paul was taking his A levels at school so she decided to stay home to keep an eye on his studying.

The flying was now pretty much routine, but the return trips were getting a little tangled. No matter how hard I tried to reduce the amount of my luggage, I'd enter the departure area loaded down with articles of any and every description – large hand-carved tribal masks, inlaid chess pieces and boards, medium-sized soapstone sculptures, woven dinner mats and massive wooden salad servers that could have doubled as shovels.

My last time through, Nairobi Immigration were becoming more than a little curious, maybe wondering if I was operating some off-the-cuff import-export trade without proper consent. One of them politely but firmly pulled me over to have a look-see. The official called over another, both appearing quite puzzled at one or two of the objects being drawn from my bag, scratching their heads in particular at a soapstone carving of a boa constrictor and a bullock locked in a primal tussle with each other. But then I don't think they ever really got it to stand the right way up. After a little more speculation, they very generously helped me gather up and re-tie most of the Nairobi wrap that had been strewn just about everywhere along the counter. And then, with a reassuring smile, they pointed me towards the exit. When I looked back over my shoulder they were still looking puzzled, trying maybe to figure out what that soapstone piece was all about.

Chapter Twelve

On returning from Kenya, there was a message waiting for me from Gerry Anderson: 'Give me a call when you get back.'

I did exactly that and, eureka, the man was on the other end of the phone.

'Shane, you've had a word with Tony about what we've got in the pipeline?'

'Yes, *Dick Spanner* – what a hoot! How far are you on with it?'

'Almost there. The first script about a human cannonball is a classic. The series could be a winner!'

'When do you want me in?'

'Tuesday next would be fine. Tony will be along too.'

'Okay, boss. Nice to see you're at it again.'

The sound studio was just about the way I remembered it, but now it was no large *Thunderbirds* ensemble number, just Gerry, Tony and the sound engineer behind the control room glass and myself in front of the microphone. Tony had harkened back to the slick-talking private eye tradition for his Dick Spanner character. That plus a kind of kookie 'film noir' camera style made Spanner a deliciously animated personality.

'Okay,' said a voice from behind the control room glass, 'it's take-off time!'

After a few stabs we decided to cut any further rehearsal time and put down the dialogue the way Tony had probably written it, off the top of his head. It was risky but would hopefully bring a feeling of spontaneity to the sessions. And maybe shave ten years off our lives as well.

But it didn't. There were a few retakes because of fumbled dialogue and the odd muffled note of hysteria, but we got it in the can and I think we got our man, Dick Spanner, right about where we wanted him. With his eccentric stop-motion animated movement, Spanner didn't so much prowl the mean streets as shift around them like a fairground dodgem car. He was probably the most lovable character I was ever associated with.

★ ★ ★

Loretta Swit was probably one of the most difficult Hollywood ladies to find a picture for. It wasn't that she was perverse, far from it, but her intense identification with Major Margaret (Hot Lips) Houlihan through the 11-year run of TV's *M*A*S*H* made it impossible for the public to think of her in any other role. But now hope was at hand. A film treatment had surfaced, not in Beverly Hills, but in a production office on London's Wardour Street and the role was that of the first woman President of the United States. The film would be titled *Whoops Apocalypse*.

Instead of Marlon Brando and Martin Sheen, the cast would be headed by Loretta Swit and her counterpart, the British Prime Minister as played by Peter Cook – that pretty well takes care of the *Whoops* factor. I read for the director, Tom Bussmann, with John Sessions alongside and secured the part of the US Secretary of State, Marvin Gelber. The story came from the pens of Andrew Marshall and David Renwick and, although there were references to the Cold War and the Falklands set-to, the farcical playing of the two leaders of the western world by Swit and Cook came uneasily close at times to another Anglo-American pairing that happened a couple of decades on.

One scene in the film called for the President (Swit) and the

Secretary of State (me) to get together for a highly confidential strategy meeting and it was decided that the only 'safe' place was aboard a privately flown helicopter over Miami. The first thing we noticed after we got ourselves seated behind the panel that divided the flight deck from the passengers was that when we closed the right-hand passenger door, it refused to stay shut. Even after several tries, it still wouldn't lock. I glanced over at Loretta, who was now savaging her second fingernail. She looked back wordlessly. Now, above us the rotor blades were starting to whirr around slowly and I quickly knocked on the panel.

'Pilot, we have a little problem back here.'

'Yeah, what is it?'

'The right-hand passenger door doesn't seem to want to lock!'

There was the slightest hint of impatience in his reply. 'Oh, that again, eh?'

'Well, maybe it's 'that again' for you but for us this is the first time and it's making us a little nervous!'

'It'll be all right, I'll tell you what to do. Close the passenger door once and then immediately once again hard. The second one should do it.'

'Where did you get this thing from, a used helicopter lot?'

'Look, you guys were lucky to pick up anything around the bay. The *Miami Vice* series has locked up just about every production facility including transport around here.'

Somebody was going to have to speak to Don Johnson about this. Anyway, I glanced again at Loretta who replied by quickly nodding towards the door. I leaned over and shut it with all the firmness I could muster and then quickly once again. It seemed to work and held with a slight 'click'.

I called out to the flight deck, 'I think it's okay, it seems to be holding all right.'

The pilot's voice came back, a trifle smug I thought. 'I told you, didn't I? Hold on, here we go!'

I turned to Loretta and patted her on the knee reassuringly. She nearly jumped a foot. We heard the rotor blades above us churning into a high-speed pattern, setting up vibrations we could feel right through the backs of our seats, and we were up and away.

Then it was time for another bulletin from up front.

'I'd keep the seat belts on, but have a look. Some view, huh?'

It was. The helicopter was now soaring up past the sheer walls of a cluster of towering city skyscrapers and the view was spellbinding. What happened next wasn't. It suddenly felt like a giant hand had reached down suddenly from the heavens and catapulted us further skyward and out of the craft's control. The pilot's voice didn't restore bags of confidence either.

'Sorry, we have a few thermals around today, it's the heat. We'll be away from them in a very short time.'

It was decidedly longer than short and then I heard a voice chanting, very close and somewhat familiar. Loretta, with features almost angelically composed, was singing the hymn 'Rock of Ages'. That almost did it for me. I had been attempting to remain a pillar of strength through all this, a haven in the midst of all the madness, and now the roles were being switched and she was trying to calm me. We hit another thermal, this one pushing us up and out on a seriously tight diagonal. Loretta and I looked at each other as if possibly for the last time as the pilot's voice filtered back a little louder and certainly a touch shakier than before.

'I think these thermals aren't going to let up. We're going back to base.'

If I could have reached him, I would have hugged him.

We somehow got through it, maybe even clasping hands at one point, and came back down to rest on the roof-top landing pad. We were a little lost for words after getting back on solid ground again. I guess a near crisis like that leaves you stuck in the middle of a vacuum with not a lot left to say. That is, until Loretta almost collapsed in great whooping gales of laughter, eyes revolving around in their sockets at the incredible nuttiness of the episode we'd just been through. Maybe all those years back-packing a medi-kit around South Korea as Hot Lips had got her used to handling just about anything. Some lady!

Another, but of quite a different nature and touch altogether, was Audrey Hepburn, who teamed up with Gregory Peck in William Wyler's blissful romantic comedy of 1953, *Roman Holiday*, about a Royal princess visiting Rome and falling in love with an investigative reporter sent to interview her. The Academy later confirmed the class of that performance by awarding Hepburn the Oscar for Best Actress of the year. The story was scripted by Dalton Trumbo, blacklisted by the 1954 McCarthy hearings on Un-American Activities and now writing under an assumed name. One does wonder, if the awards committee had known of the writer's true identity, whether the Best Actress Oscar would still have gone to Miss Hepburn.

The original film was never going to be bettered, but the studios kept trying. The 1987 remake moved the location to Lisbon, as Rome was now too busy and expensive for a 'remake' budget. To replace Peck and Eddie Albert, his reporter sidekick, they brought in Tom Conti and Ed Begley Jr. The latter had just finished filming *Amazon Women on the Moon* and was badly in need of some therapy. The light comic tale of *Roman Holiday* looked a possible answer. One of the young stars of NBC's *Dynasty*, Catherine Oxenberg, assumed the role of the princess. I was taken onto the pay roll as Hogan, the managing editor who commissions Conti to secure an interview with the visiting European princess come hell or high water. That done, cast, crew and a tier of producers packed their bags and headed for Portugal.

Lisbon is an entrancing capital city, has a broad, palm-lined central avenue and the required near-tropical climate, but it is not Rome. So out went the second unit to bring back the needed exterior shots of the Colosseum, the Trevi Fountain, St Marco and the Via Veneto. And presto! we were in the midst of the Eternal City.

It wasn't an easy assignment for Tom Conti but he was terrific on and off screen, and if the film hadn't been up against the original, it could well have had far greater impact. Ed Begley seemed well on the way through his recovery, but another disaster popped up when he was informed that the roof of his San Fernando Valley home had just blown off in a freak thunderstorm. He was on the phone at every break in the shooting, checking on the water damage, seeing to it the new roof was going on the right way around and if the tiles were still flying off and clogging up his neighbour's pool. At the end of two weeks, the accounting department was putting in a claim for another adding machine to replace the original, which had broken down under the spiralling charges of his marathon telephone conversations. I don't think the production office minded that much. As kooky as he was sometimes liable to get, Begley had a habit of lighting up pictures wherever he went.

Two days later, with our Rome-Lisbon holiday over and in the can, it was back to packing and getting ready to leave for home. I was half way out of my hotel room door when the telephone buzzed. I pulled my luggage back in and picked up the receiver. Ah, my trusty agent, popping up again.

'Hey, you're still out there?

'Guess so, I'm on the other end of the line.'

'Oh, right – look, I've got you a week on a Mario Puzo mini-series shooting in Budapest – interested?'

'If it's in Budapest – any time. What's it about?'

'Italian immigrants landing in New York before the Second World War.'

'My Italiano is not all that good.'

'That's okay, they want you to play an Irish-born cop by the name of Reilly, okay?'

'With the name I've got, sure. When do I suit up?'

'Pretty soon – near the end of the week. By the way, the star is Sophia Loren.'

'My wife's going to divorce me.'

Mario Puzo is of course best known as the author of the bestselling novel *The Godfather*. But there had been one before that, according to him, was infinitely better written. It was about the life of Italian immigrants during and after the Depression in New York and the central character of the book, Lucia Santa, was based on Puzo's own mother. The book was called *The Fortunate Pilgrim* and this was the character to be portrayed by Sophia Loren.

My first filming call wasn't on the board for another two days, which gave me an opportunity to drop in on some of Budapest's exceptional sights that I'd missed the first time around. I lined them up, checked to see my wallet had some reasonable identification, remembered to keep it out of my hip pocket and set off. The first day's pickings were the grand State Opera House, so splendidly situated, overlooking the sweep of the Danube and still bearing the unmistakable birth traces of its Renaissance upbringing, and St Stephen's Basilica, where if you really wanted to, and by dropping a few Hungarian 'forint' coins in the pot, you could get to view the mummified glass-encased hand of St Stephen, the country's patron saint. Then as a relaxing aftermath, a wander over the cobble-stoned streets to any of the city's 80 hot thermal baths for a luxurious dousing and a floating game of chess on the side, if you could keep the sweat out of your eyes.

Just off the central area of the city, a stretch of wartime ghetto quarters had been transformed by the design team into a block of Lower East Side tenements, where the newly arrived Italian immigrants would have first settled in. The street was crammed with outdoor market stalls, trinket sellers, NYC fire hydrants and people filling up their shopping baskets. This was Sergeant Reilly's patch, where he walked his beat each day. Being an immigrant like themselves, although from a different side of the world, he could move among the Italians easily, exchanging hellos and conversations with whomever he came across. And this was the way it was filmed, loose and 'au naturelle' with very little formatting.

Then there was the signora, Lucia Santa. Even in a homespun dress, rough stockings and bulky brogues, Loren seemed to absorb even the slightest sliver of light and return it sevenfold. She glowed. We shared a few sidewalk pleasantries, talked of the arrangements for an upcoming immigrant's meeting and the behaviour of some young tenement toughs who might be headed for trouble with the police, and that was about it. Maybe just as well – if you gazed at her long enough, you were apt to forget your own name, let alone what the conversation was supposed to be about.

Grim as those hard early years of cooped-up tenement living must have been, they produced a freedom of spirit that was unquenchable. They were on their own, friends and families had been left behind, they could only depend on each other and whatever the misfortune or adversity, they would face up to it and that would hold them together. That's the spirit that Puzo was writing about and that's what was felt in every part of the story. Film can sometimes opt for the shallow and frivolous, this one presented the human spirit in its glories and frailties in an uncompromising, greatly inspired way.

It was an exceptional visit – but then it always is in Budapest.

★ ★ ★

Back home, our three sons were now branching out in three different directions. Damian had graduated from St Mary's College with an arts degree and then moved into a computer graphics firm.

Ben, on his hours away from the London College of Printing, had been apprenticing himself to a New York photographer and old family friend called Frank Monaco. Each time they'd get together, Frank would hand Ben a photo assignment somewhere around London. It didn't matter how he got the shots, as long as they were taken in black and white and they were delivered back on time. On one Monaco mission, he had to talk his way onto a police river launch, only to discover they were on their way to dredge up a drowned body that had been lying half submerged in the Thames for some weeks. Quite soon after that, thanking his mentor for the experience, Ben joined a production house in Soho as a runner, then graduated to their location-finding team in very short order, deciding that he would spend the rest of his career firmly on dry land.

Paul, the youngest, was following Damian at St Mary's College in Twickenham, preparing for a course in higher education. I somehow had a feeling that he might well end up somewhere in the visual and filmic side of things, or maybe not. Time would tell.

Then something unbelievable, almost unthinkable, occurred. Granada TV called with an offer to rejoin *Coronation Street.*

Not only had I appeared in the series 18 years before as a completely different character, Joe Donelli, but after fleeing a charge of murdering fellow American airman Steve Tanner and holding Stan Ogden hostage in Minnie Caldwell's flat, I had turned a gun on myself and shot my brains out !

It was a near out-of-body experience to resurface as another character after a finale like that. This time I was scripted in as Malcolm Reid, a 'some time ago' romantic partner of Audrey Roberts, proprietress of the local corner shop. Reid was now back living in Canada with his son Stephen, the result of his and Audrey's brief but torrid relationship. He returns to England and takes Audrey for a 'heart to heart' weekend in Blackpool, where they both come to realise that a rekindling of the fires has long passed.

It created quite a stir among the public, who let their objections be known by letter and phone that a former convicted murderer who had then killed himself should not be allowed back into *Coronation Street* cast even in a new guise.

Chapter Thirteen

He was the first person I sighted as I entered the TV studio – but then it would have been hard to miss him, for all the electricity was still there. I stepped towards him, hand outstretched, wondering if he'd remember back to 20 years before.

'It's been a long time, Ray.'

'I'll say. Korea, wasn't it?'

'Yep, off the coast of Pusan, the south-east tip.'

'That was some war. It's good to see you.'

We'd both been aboard the USS destroyer *Pueblo* during the early 1950s bloodbath between North and South Korea. Not the real thing, but a reconstruction for a Granada TV documentary about one of the most incendiary incidents of that calamitous war. There was a marginal difference in our ranks – I was on board as an ordinary rating while Ray McAnally wore the insignia of Commander. He looked like he could still handle it.

Over the previous ten years, along with very special performances at the Abbey Theatre in Dublin, he had moved dramatically into the international film market, picking up both *Evening Standard* and BAFTA awards for his role as Cardinal Altamirano in *The Mission*, a second top award for his performance in Le Carré's *A Perfect Spy*, and with a posthumous blue ribbon yet to come for his role as Daniel Day-Lewis' father in the Oscar-winning *My Left Foot*.

Now we were clocking in for another contentious production, the Channel 4 series *A Very British Coup*, with McAnally as newly elected

Labour Prime Minister Harry Perkins, who proposes to dissolve all newspaper monopolies, oust every American base on UK soil, and give full backing to unilateral nuclear disarmament. Right-wing operators with the covert support of the United States immediately launch a campaign to stop him. I was in the mix as Marcus Morgan, his strongest supporter and, ironically, a high-profile member of the US government as Secretary of State. Perkins might just need him.

McAnally was staggeringly convincing in his role as a statesman who, despite the forces ranged against him, never compromises his principles. But then he was that way in real life, too. Unfortunately, that life ended all too soon; Ray died just a year after the first broadcast of *A Very British Coup*, aged 63. During our time on the series he invited me over to his home in Ireland to play a few rounds of golf and dig out a few old Irish ballads to sing together – he had a fine tenor voice. The regret that we didn't have a chance to do either of these things is still there.

★ ★ ★

Early in 1989 a call came in, all brisk and business-like, from my present agent.

'Ever been to Berlin?' he asked.

He rarely spent too much time enquiring about the state of your health, figuring that if you were able to lift the receiver, you were still of this world and therefore all things were possible.

'Well you're not exactly going to Berlin,' he added. 'You're going back to Budapest, which they've made look very much like Berlin before the Second World War.'

'This sounds like a film scenario, could I be right?'

'Well, almost. It's an NBC mini-series based on a bestseller about the lead-up years to World War II. William Shirer's *The Nightmare Years*.'

'You're getting better, Rupert.'

'Yes, I thought you might like it. And you're once again occupying the US ambassadorial suite. Just during shooting hours of course.'

Sam Waterston, Marthe Keller from *Marathon Man* and Kurtwood Smith (cast as Joseph Goebbels) were the main players in this look at Hitler's ominous power-grab in Berlin and the terrifying, global consequences. Waterston was William Shirer himself, the 'fist in a velvet glove' American editor of an English-speaking Berlin newspaper whose voice was one of the very few raised in protest at the growing horror of day-to-day Nazi atrocities. He wrote 20 books, became, like Edward R Murrow, one of the pioneering radio commentators, warned of the approachng Holocaust and, also like Murrow, was a great friend of Mahatma Gandhi. Of course, both Shirer and Murrow were subpoena'd by the House Un-American Activities Committee.

The role that lodged me in the ambassadorial suite again was that of the leading representative of the US government in Germany, George Dodd. Though a born in-fighter, he was persistently stymied by his government's insistence that he play a neutral role in the interests of the White House. Editor Shirer and ambassador Dodd, both of them constrained by US government directives, therefore formed themselves into a deep and determined alliance.

Budapest was becoming the preferred choice of many production companies searching for suitably lived-in war (and pre-war) locations around Europe. The city's architecture displayed styles as diverse as Italian, Prussian, French and Spanish, lending Budapest a climate of mystery and intrigue that you came to sense around every corner. To top it off, the studio facilities were up and running, with a technical force that rated with some of the most highly regarded on the continent. The ghostly presences of such shadowy 'agents provocateur' as Peter Lorre, Sydney Greenstreet and Conrad Veidt (remember them?) all added up to an irresistible mix.

On my first night's walk around Budapest, a voice called out from an outdoor café down near the edge of the Danube. I looked around and there was Sam Waterston, sitting alone at a table with a waiter ladling a very red and very thick liquid into his soup bowl. I hadn't seen him since we'd managed to escape blowing ourselves up in the BBC series *Oppenheimer*, which was filmed in the American west nine years previously and concerned the development of the atomic bomb.

I sat down alongside and shook hands. He gestured to the giant soup tureen covering most of the centre of the table.

'Have some, it's really delicious.'

I took a look at the rather lumpy mix in his bowl – paddling through it would have been a problem.

'You sure there's no underwater life swimming around in there?'

'Haven't come across any yet,' he said, licking his lips.

The waiter returned to tip the tureen and I had my first taste of Hungarian Borscht. It was mouth-watering – a rich medley of earthy vegetable tastes topped with glistening slices of beetroot. I'd arrived! I had some more.

The next day the director, Anthony Page, took us into the centre of Budapest where red, black and white banners of the Reichstag were already hanging from roof to sidewalk over many of the city's main municipal buildings. The present-day Hungarians must have loved that. They had already suffered through two successive occupations, first by the Germans in 1944 and then the Russians in 1956, and now it appeared they were getting into the middle of another. Many parts of the city centre still bore open testimony to the savage battering the capital had suffered during, first, the Nazi occupation and then the anti-Stalinist uprising which provoked the Russian take-over. A few buildings remained just shells of their former grandeur; others carried deep pit marks from heavy mortar and tank fire. What this did was to turn back the hands of history and give us a taste of the incendiary times the Hungarians must have lived through. War is truly a bitch.

It turned out to be a pretty tough shoot, the designer having arranged matters so that each new set was reached only after scaling some of the longest and steepest spiral staircases I'd ever set foot on. Mind you, they led up into some immensely eye-opening areas –

chandelier-lit landings, rows of spacious, oak-panelled offices and libraries that would keep you perched there for weeks. Happily, the stairs also went downwards and on many a tasty evening we would troop down their marble widths into some of old Budapest's finest and most gracious dining salons. There we'd be greeted formally by waiters in white tie and tails and shown to our candle-lit table accompanied by music from a classical string quartet. The meal probably cost little more than double the price of a twin hamburger special with 'fries' at the newly opened McDonald's down the street.

The NBC network got the film and the authenticity they wanted, due in large part to Anthony Page's direction but maybe even more to all the local actors and citizens, whose weathered Magyar features lent a shattering reality to the unfolding story. They were 'being' and not assuming characters; true grit was never in short supply around Budapest.

My last view of the wide-running Danube, its lamp-lit bridges, the beautifully sculptured façades of its palaces and villas perched high on Buda's east hillside, lingered with me all the way back to the touchdown at Heathrow. It had suddenly dawned on me how fond I'd grown of Budapest and the people who lived there. I'd even learned enough Hungarian to say 'Good morning', 'How much is your beetroot?' and 'What's the best way to Salzburg?' Hungarian has long been recognised as the most difficult language in the world to assimilate, which is possibly why they're the world's most formidable linguists. To them, every other language must seem like a piece of cake. Its only known link is with Finnish, though the difficulty is that they rarely find themselves within speaking distance of each other.

★ ★ ★

Canon Arthur Payton was really the only one to do it. He had married Sheila and I back in 1963 and now, nearly 30 years later, son Ben and his beautiful and very Irish bride-to-be Catherine were about to tie the knot in one of the most renowned houses of worship in Dublin – the 16th century chapel in the grounds of Trinity College. The privilege was granted only to those who had graduated 'cum laude' from the university, and they accepted the honour with little delay and great gratitude.

As soon as that was arranged, Ben put in a phone call to the Reverend Arthur Payton at Grange House in Norfolk to see if he would consider a first-class flight to Dublin and four-star accommodation in order to officiate at the wedding. For the second time in three decades the Canon unhesitatingly agreed to preside over a Rimmer marriage. He arrived in Dublin along with a multitude of our family friends, relatives and well-wishers whose numbers could have taken over the town. Some began their celebrations on the eve of the wedding with a few stops along one of Dublin's famous 'pub streets' – the flow of Guinness was almost tidal.

The next day's wedding proceeded beautifully, the Reverend Payton's nuptial blessings filled the hearts of everyone there, and as he escorted Ben and Catherine to sign the register, he nodded over my cue to sing 'Panis Angelicus'. At the end of the ceremony – as the guests approached the Great Hall where the celebratory dinner was to be held, presided over by our new-found in-laws, Kieran and Annetta McGuire – a beautiful, auburn-haired harpist played and sang a full Gaelic welcome. As dusk fell, the newly-weds boarded a horse-drawn carriage outside Trinity College and, to the cheers and shouts of a happy and exhilarated throng, sped off into the night. It was a wedding that none of us is liable to forget.

Midway through the next week a call came in from director Annie Castledine. Annie, a very vital theatre lady, was about to mount a Chichester revival of one of the classiest and wackiest stage comedies ever written, *Arsenic and Old Lace*, in which two elderly Brooklyn sisters poison various unfortunates while their delusional brother Teddy digs what he thinks is the Suez canal, but is in fact a mass graveyard, in the cellar.

I was to read for the investigating Lieutenant Rooney, who by the end of this macabre tale is ready for a straitjacket himself. Would I come along to meet Annie in her flat in St John's Wood? Bernard Bresslaw, Rosemary Harris, Peter Davison, Elizabeth Spriggs and Geoffrey Freshwater were already on board – and after the meeting so, happily, was I. Rehearsals would start in a week's time in London.

Next morning I was hanging onto a dream of taking an extra bow after an exhilarating Chichester performance and not wanting to wake out of it. But then I did and the feeling couldn't have been worse. Something terribly heavy seemed to be strapped to my chest and, no matter which way I moved, I couldn't shift out from under it. I lay there for a few more minutes trying to figure out what was going on. Things got a little better but not much. I reached across and tapped Sheila lightly on the shoulder. She turned towards me sleepily.

'You're lying in late – what's the matter?'

'Do I have something sitting on my chest?'

Her eyes were wide open now.

'How's the breathing?'

'Not great.'

'For how long?'

'Since I woke up.'

'Is it getting any better?'

'Yes, a little, yes.'

'Can you get dressed?'

'Yes, I think so. Why – where are we going?'

'First to the clinic, to see Basya Howells.'

Basya, who was our local doctor and dear friend, took one look at me and told Sheila to get me to Barnet Hospital as quickly as she could. She would phone ahead for us. At the hospital, they stretched me out on an examination table and then poked, prodded and photographed everything they could reach. Half an hour later, one of the cardiac department doctors came by with a first diagnosis – a faulty artery looked to be the problem and they were going to get me to Harefield heart hospital as soon as an ambulance became available. It was then decided that, to get there more quickly, we would drive the 15 miles ourselves. On the way out I noticed the cardiologist whispering something to Sheila, then a brief flash of apprehension crossed her face.

As we turned onto the highway I asked her, 'What did the doctor have to say on the way out?'

She slowed the car for a moment and turned to me. 'He said he wouldn't be surprised if they had to do open-heart surgery when we get to Harefield.' She looked at me a little closer. 'Are you all right?'

'I've felt better.'

She nodded gently and pressed her foot on the accelerator. We didn't talk much after that.

A cardiac team led by two Irish doctors, whom I mistook for interns they appeared so impossibly youthful, immediately took over. An artery problem was ruled out; instead they found the trouble to be viral pericarditis, an infection of the protective membrane around the heart. The area had to be drained immediately. That's when the fun fair started. To do the job, they had to drop a drainage tube down my throat. Though more than half sedated, I rallied all my resources to repel the attack as if defending the Alamo, and with about as much success. Just before the anaesthetic took hold I slung out a wild right hand, tagging one of them on the ear, then I turned as meek as a lamb. The first syphoning took off two quarts of liquid that shouldn't have been there.

One of the doctors looked over from jotting something down on the log sheet.

'Well, we're off to a pretty good start,' he said, 'but there's more of that to get rid of. You're going to be around here for a little while yet. Best thing is to relax as much as you can and don't worry about things.'

It very much looked like the curtain was coming down before it even went up on my first date at Chichester. I looked up at Sheila.

'Better phone Annie and tell her she'd better look for another lieutenant.'

Sheila glanced over to the doctor, who nodded apologetically in agreement.

But Annie, bless her, wouldn't have it. She wasn't about to replace me until there was no possible chance that I could show up. But, willing as she was, how was she going to cover for the London rehearsals that were due to start in two days' time? The play called for a lot of quick-fire dialogue between the lieutenant and his two aides and the pace would have to be nudging the speed limit.

Next afternoon I was lying on my hospital bed, trying to lose myself in the sports pages, when there was a knock on the door and in came Corey Johnson and his buddy Joe Alessi, otherwise known as officers Klein and Brophy, Lieutenant Rooney's two investigative assistants. If Mohammed couldn't come to the mountain, then the mountain would come to Mohammed.

Corey was carrying about the largest armful of flowers I think I'd ever seen, Joe was hugging a briefcase as if it contained the crown jewels – well, not quite, just the complete rehearsal script for *Arsenic and Old Lace*, with stage comments scrawled on the side by the amazing Annie Castledine. It took one helluva pause before I was able to look up at both of them.

'Annie must think I'm going to make it in time.'

'She does,' answered Corey. 'We all do.'

He placed the flowers on the bedside table, which pretty well covered any sight or sound of the conversation from the other two patients in the small ward. There were a few yips and chuckles from around the bedside, but in between a complete going-over of our scenes in the script. It was totally bizarre and would help, I felt, to speed up my recovery. That evening the late rounds doctor, after checking the nurse's comments for the day, looked down at me in some puzzlement.

'Those two visitors you had this afternoon...' He paused and I feared the worst. There would be no more bedside rehearsal, I thought; Joe and Corey would be locked out! 'They must have been a real tonic for you,' he added. 'Your day's results are really quite good!'

He walked to the doorway, then turned around to me.

'But we've still got a problem with your temperature.'

So the infection had been somewhat lessened, but the temperature was still too far above normal. As long as that remained so, I wouldn't be going anywhere.

Joe and Corey dropped in one more time, getting us through a double reading of our scenes before having to leave to join the rest of the cast on its way to Chichester. They paused at the side of the bed and handed me the slightly tattered rehearsal script.

'Might be better to keep this under your pillow – and we'll see you down there.'

'Thanks guys. That'll be something nice to think about.'

I watched them go, wondering how the odds were stacked that we'd ever get the chance to convert our in-hospital rehearsals into the real thing on stage.

The ward doctor passed them on the way in.

'Are those the two who've been helping with your convalescence?'

'Yes – wonderful, isn't it, how a friendly chat will buck you up.'

'Surprising,' he answered, referring back to his chart. 'Well, the infection does seem to be easing up a little, but your temperature has a way to drop yet, I'm afraid.'

His response seemed to leave an opening – I took it.

'Would you be open to a proposition?'

'What do you mean?'

'If my temperature drops to say one degree above normal, and everything else on the chart looks okay, would it be possible to rejoin the cast at Chichester?'

A wisp of an Irish smile came across his face.

'That's where your two visitors are from, isn't it?'

'They were on a mission of mercy, Doc.'

'Let's see how it goes.'

Heartening, but how could there possibly be the time to reduce my temperature enough? I experienced an empty few minutes until I remembered from a long time back an elderly Scottish GP and naturopath called Dr Latto, who used to attend us as a family from his surgery in Reading. He was a fine medical gentleman and the whole family prospered under his care. He was the doctor who kept Francis Chichester's cancer at bay without the use of chemotherapy, allowing him to make his one-man voyage around the world in his 16-foot sloop, *Gypsy Moth*. The good doctor had also, some time before, cured me of a perilously high temperature by prescribing a clove of garlic to be held in the mouth during sleep and any other time if the people around could bear it. The temperature drop had been dramatic. I immediately phoned Sheila and asked her to smuggle in a cluster.

Annie had asked Sheila to telephone every day to keep her up to date on how things were going. When Sheila reported that I had asked her to bring in some cloves of garlic, there was rather a long pause before Annie replied.

'Is that a good sign or bad?"

'I'll have to let you know – but it's from a good source.'

'I'm afraid, Sheila, the management is getting anxious about our missing lieutenant. I don't think I can stall them past Thursday. Believe me, I'm sorry.'

'Annie, what you've done so far has been magnificent. I'll phone tomorrow. Right now I've got to go out and find some garlic! Bless you.'

The garlic began to work, though I probably tried to spit most of it out during the night. With only two days to go, my temperature had dropped a degree and a half. That fine doctor's advice had blessedly hit the target. I remembered him once saying, 'Truth is everything, it is all that matters – I would never prescribe anything other; that and faith are all you need.'

By Wednesday morning my temperature had dropped another two degrees. Even the hospital doctor was becoming cautiously optimistic, though a little mystified. There would be a final check-up on Thursday morning and, if all was well, Sheila and I would be on our way. That night I inserted an extra clove.

Holding our breaths, the morning check proved A-okay across the board, even the temperature was nudging normal. After promising to do everything in moderation and thanking the doctors and nurses with what we hoped expressed the full gratitude we truly felt, we drove out through the gates waving a final goodbye.

The message we sent down to the theatre was short and sweet: 'We're on our way.'

The whole company came out to greet our arrival that day. But, great as it was to be back on the open road, I wasn't yet aware how much my stay at Harefield had taken out of me. It would take some perseverance not to teeter too noticeably once the rehearsal action heated up on stage. For a while I think they were considering pushing me on as a kind of wheel-chaired Attorney Ironside, but luckily the juices began to flow more freely again and by the second week Officer Rooney was on his feet, twirling his baton and playing it as writ.

From late April to early July of 1991, *Arsenic and Old Lace* proved one of the smash successes of the season at the Chichester Festival Theatre; in fact, it only missed being transferred to the West End because no theatre was available at the time we needed it. Annie and the whole company were very disappointed the transfer hadn't been made. I, however, deemed myself exceptionally lucky just to have been a part of that glorious Chichester summer.

Chapter Fourteen

And so away from the balm of the Sussex countryside and a turn back to the grit and grind of pre-rush-hour traffic massing in both directions along London's North Circular Road. I was heading for Twickenham Studios and a meeting with Renny Rye, the director designate for a new –

Damn! The VW engine in the rear of the Camper gave a gut-wrenching groan, almost a sob, then a wheeze, then two pathetic hiccups and went silent. So did I. I glanced at my watch. The meeting was due in 25 minutes, and it was to be considered for a new Dennis Potter TV series called *Lipstick On Your Collar*.

Potter was now top of the heap of a very impressive bunch of English TV writers. It was an automatic feather in your cap to be included in anything he produced, and here I was grounded by the side of the North Circular, which was not only the most frantically paced stretch of asphalt around London, but one that offered the sparsest kind of public service to get you out of trouble. Holding my breath, I turned the ignition key a millimetre at a time – absolute zero. I know as much about a VW rear-combustion engine as I do about the Rosetta stone but, unfazed, I slid out the driver's door, trying not to get sucked into the hot draught of traffic whizzing past about two feet away, and opened up the engine. At least I knew where that was.

The release of hot air almost buckled me. I gave it a minute, cowering beside the back end of the van, then peered in, giving everything a turn or a tap that looked as if it could do with it, then tested the oil level which looked okay. I dug around a little more, succeeding in scraping off an ugly stockpile of grease, oil and grime, which I then managed to spread thoroughly across my shirt and grey flannels. Things were now going from bad to hopeless until I noticed a length of corrugated tubing about two inches wide, dangling from the open end of what I discovered later was the air filter. I eased the tubing up around it as far as it would go, prayed a little and then headed back towards the driver's seat. If this didn't work, goodbye Dennis Potter, so long *Lipstick On Your Collar.*

I re-inserted the ignition key and slowly turned it. The engine sputtered once, coughed and then held. I quietly apologised to VW for all the unkind things I had been thinking about them, inched back into the flow of traffic and, with a heartbeat that was coming down from plus extra to near normal, headed west for the Twickenham Studios turn-off.

Twenty minutes later I was following director Renny Rye up the flight of stairs from reception to his office on the first floor. Inside, instead of offering a chair, he fixed me with a penetrating gaze that went from my head, down across my grease- and sweat-streaked shirt to the tops of my worn and noticeably scuffed shoes. After this, he turned, went around behind his desk, sat down and then gestured me to take a seat. Although he appeared utterly charming, it was beginning to make me a little nervous that he hadn't said one damn thing since we entered his office. Except for the stare, there hadn't been a lot happening between us.

I decided to try breaking the ice.

'Would you like me to read something?'

'No, I don't think so, unless you want to.'

The conversation was heading for the surreal.

'I guess I'm too late, is that it? I'm sorry, but...'

'No, not at all – it's that you're not required to.'

The penny finally dropped.

'You mean...?'

'I mean you don't need to. Dennis wants you for the role. He just wanted me to check that you looked all right for the Colonel Trekker part. I'm happy with that, okay?'

'Delighted, I'm delighted.'

It suddenly struck me how I must have appeared in my grime-streaked shirt and trousers.

'Sorry for the state of my clothes. I was tussling with a car engine before I got here.'

'That's okay. Trekker was probably that kind of character anyway.'

At the door I said, 'Give my regards to the Man, will you?'

'We'll send you on a script. Rehearsals start next week.'

I had been in the Potter fold once before, in the heart-warming 1985 film *Dreamchild*, the story of Alice Liddell, who in her 80th year was discovered to have been, as a child, the model for Lewis Carroll's *Alice in Wonderland*. Not believing in doing things by halves, an American radio station brought her to New York and seated her in an open convertible Lincoln limousine for a ticker-tape parade along Broadway. I played the station owner, who saw the publicity value of the event but who wouldn't have known *Alice in Wonderland* from *Annie Get Your Gun*.

Director Gavin Millar had chosen Coral Browne, one of the grande dames of the British theatre, to portray the octogenarian Alice, while Ian Holm played Lewis Caroll. Coral Browne was exquisite in character as a 'full of wonder' 80-year-old Alice, but could be quite sparky away from it. When asked where her husband, Vincent Price, was at the time, she answered mischievously, 'Getting his teeth pointed for his next role.'

I now joined the line-up along with Ewan McGregor, Douglas Henshall, Roy Hudd, Louise Germaine, Giles Thomas and Peter Jeffrey for the first episode of *Lipstick On Your Collar*. Following two weeks of line and movement drills in a nearby rehearsal room, we moved into Twickenham's ground floor studio where *Lipstick* would be shot. Dennis Potter would be up in his first floor office, working on further episodes of the script.

By this time he was suffering badly from psoriatic anthropathy, which caused continual and painful peeling of the skin and an advancing paralysis of the joints. Both his hands had now closed into fists and he was unable to work with his typewriter, but somehow carried on writing by hand. We were not told about the severity of his condition until halfway through the series. There was not one of us plying his lines on the floor below who was unmindful of the courage of the man. We were determined to get the play right for him.

The production was slowly finding its feet, marked most afternoons by Renny climbing the stairs to the first floor during tea break then reappearing a short time later with a sheaf of scribbled notes bearing Potter's observations on the day's playing. Pithy is slightly understating the tone of them, but they were always pertinent and always helpful. Except for one time when he honed in on me after offering complimentary comments to just about everyone else.

'Shane,' he said, 'you mis-read the speech about the chickens!'

'I was just trying to make the quotation right, Dennis. I've known it since I was a kid.'

'And you say the quotation is?'

I sensed a gathering roll of thunder under the question – but if you're going to get wet you might as well get soaked.

'The saying is 'When the chickens come home to roost,' not 'rest'.'

There was a silence which seemed to last an eternity.

'You're sure about that?'

'Absolutely sure – I wouldn't have mentioned it otherwise.'

'All right. But, just to let you know, you're the first actor I've ever allowed to change one word in any of my scripts!'

He turned and walked away, gnarled hands deep in his pockets. After a few steps he paused and looked back at me.

'But thanks for telling me.'

Despite Potter's sometimes cranky exterior, everyone involved in *Lipstick On Your Collar* became absolutely devoted to him, whether actor, director, crew-member or producer. I had never been a part of such a deep and open-hearted giving as happened during the filming of *Lipstick*. His presence at the final wrap party, even though in intense discomfort, gratified everyone gathered – it was all that any of us could have wished for.

★ ★ ★

What a box of tricks this business can be. The front door of a house in Munich opens and, that established, you film the remainder of the scene on a set at Pinewood. And the audience will swear it's still all taking place behind that door in Munich. It's very often a case of budget economics or because the original setting of the story – Paris, London, Rome etc, would have far too many traffic and local council restrictions to make the filming workable.

You cover a lot of territory, some of it real, some the product of a set designer's worldly-wise imagination. Over the past years I had strolled through an old quarter of Lisbon pretending it was part of the Trevi Fountain area of Rome, and walked the beat along cobbled streets in Budapest, magically transformed into a 1920s Brooklyn tenement district. And now here was a hi-tech thriller set miles up in space, filmed in 1995 on the pastoral green turf of old Ireland.

It had all started in a roadside diner off the main east-bound highway out of Las Vegas, Nevada. Two men – one of them Stuart Gordon, who had directed the horror hit *Re-Animator*, and the other a writer friend called Ted Mann – were seated at a window table looking out at the passing road haulage traffic bound for the big city depots of Chicago, Detroit and New York. It was around 11 o'clock at night and pitch black; about all that was discernible out on the road were the powerful headlight probes of the heavy-duty juggernauts, the twinkling smaller lights outlining the drivers' cabs and the glint of the massive steel verticals on the front-mounted grills between them. It was an almost hallucinatory sight. Gordon commented later that he just said to his friend, 'Some sight. You know, it's almost as if this could be happening out in space!'

'And that could maybe make a story,' Mann replied.

A few hours later, Gordon sketched out a rough scenario, dropped in a bevy of bizarre characters and handed it over to Mann, who then converted it into a screenplay. And so *Space Truckers* was launched. Because of *Re-Animator*'s success, Gordon was able to contract the services of Dennis Hopper and Stephen Dorff as the space pilots on the deck of Hopper's freelance cargo-liner. Charles Dance brought along his most villianous persona as the horribly disfigured psychopath Macanudo and I signed on as the egomaniac Corporate Chief of one of the most powerful multi-nationals in space, who spends most of his time careening through the universe in a rocket-powered limo, keeping close tabs on his string of intergalactic holdings. Name: E J Saggs. Usual attire: dazzling silver jodhpurs with the circumference of a tent and shiny black, knee-high stormtrooper boots.

Cinéma vérité it wasn't – not even close.

There was a faded elegance about the Ardmore Studios, situated just south of Dublin and the Wicklow Mountains, where most of the filming would take place. The studio was owned at the time by the rock group U2, who were zipping around the world on tour and not bothering too much about the leaking eaves, missing roof tiles or a little subsidence here and there in their acquired studios back home. It was about the most lived-in old film facility ever and it was slightly ironic that it was now the base of operations for a madcap futuristic space adventure.

Dennis Hopper had all the grit needed for the lead role of a feisty freelance space trucker and had a made-to-measure sidekick in Steven Dorff, who in a haunting and unaccountable way evoked memories of a young Humphrey Bogart. We had several tough scenes together and none of us backed up an inch.

Hopper seemed to shy away from socialising most of the time, but there were exceptions. Once when we got out for a few holes of golf at the Royal Dublin course, which was a delight and where I witnessed up close that legendary determination of his, thundering the ball up to 250 yards out from the tee. There was another occasion when singer Van Morrison came along at Hopper's invitation to have lunch at the studio. A lot of cutlery came to rest at other tables as the two of them sat down to truly enjoy each other's company. Two legends, showbusiness warriors both. Awesome!

★ ★ ★

'Hey Shane! It's Ed Bishop. I've got some news for you.'

It was 1996, and Ed Bishop – an old friend and, in an alternate existence, Commander Ed Straker of the *UFO* series – was on the phone with his monthly nuggets of news.

Ed was a kind of archivist compiler of just about every item that could connect with the interests of North American actors living in London; eg, what prospective productions would soon be surfacing, which ones to go for and which ones to avoid, depending on who he was talking to. He also dealt with side issues like who was feuding with whom and who was making up, who had broken a leg and was suing, who was about to leave our fair community by returning to North America, and who looked sadly likely to be taking the trip upward to the great casting suite in the sky.

I'm not sure if even he knew how he got into this position, but there was little doubt he had an uncanny knack of selecting from the flow of rumour and hype those items that could be of advantage to his fellow actors, and he was immensely generous with the information. But on with the phone call!

'I've just had a preliminary meeting with the casting director at the National Theatre. They're about to produce Arthur Miller's *Death of a Salesman*. I dropped in a word for you. You'd be great for Charlie; you know, Willie Loman's best friend.'

'Terrific. What about you, what are you up for?' I asked.

'Uncle Ben, a kind of ghostly character, nice.'

'They're in about the same age group, aren't they?'

'Yeah, I guess so, but I think you'd be better as Charlie.'

'Who's playing the lead, Willie Loman?'

'Alun Armstrong. Do you know him?'

'Only as part of his admiring audience. Has a voice that could crunch a Brinks Security truck!'

'That's him.'

'It would be great getting together on this one, Ed. Thanks.'

I passed the news on to my agent, who in his brisk, on-the-ball fashion, contacted the National Theatre. And by the end of the week I was back at the South Bank as a player.

London couldn't seem to get enough of Arthur Miller and Miller, it appeared, held the same fondness for London. Whenever he was deemed fit enough, he would hop onto an American Airlines flight and turn up at a theatre that 'just happened' to be performing one of his plays. There was bound to be one somewhere. The only things that might get in the way of these trans-Atlantic hops was a chronic back ailment and his deep and abiding love for his lakeside house in Westchester County just outside New York.

He not only happened to be an audience favourite but an actor's one as well. It's not often that a writer is able to pick up the sounds and rhythms of life in side-street New York and transcribe them 'livingly' onto a page of script, or for that matter, to log the day to day struggles and triumphs that come with living there, then raise them to such a soaring dramatic level as Arthur Miller could. *A View from the Bridge*, *All My Sons* and *Broken Glass* had all appeared fairly recently in London's West End and played to packed audiences. Now, it was again the turn of *Death of a Salesman*, for which Miller had won the Pulitzer Prize in 1947.

Paul Muni had performed Willie Loman on Broadway, then Fredric March had followed with a towering performance on film. Now it was the time for Alun Armstrong to stake his place on the stage of the National Theatre. Mark Strong, Marjorie Yates and Corey Johnson were brought in by the director David Thacker to round out the Loman family. Arthur Miller, who was in Salzburg attending a symposium at the time, brought them all over for a week's tuition in New York pace and patter. It paid off. After a month's intensive rehearsal back at the National we were ready to place *Salesman* on the Lyttleton Theatre stage. The production came out a winner, playing for six months in London, then enjoyed capacity weeks in Manchester, Leeds, Nottingham and Glasgow.

From the beginning, Ed and I shared a dressing room. This can sometimes be a chancy arrangement but here it was a pure delight, spiced with his nightly off-stage choruses of every cowboy ballad in the book from 'Red River Valley' to '16 Tons'. At times some of the front row audiences must have reckoned the theatre's audio system had strayed into the BBC's Country and Western slot, but they seemed quite happy to go along with it until curtain up.

The play received bouquets on each stop of the tour. Alun's final walk away from the audience into the darkness of the rear stage produced that total hush in the theatre that one can only yearn for. Then the audience would erupt into a rocking, thunderous ovation which was the only fitting response to Alun's playing of that leading role and the production that accompanied it. It was a great time. It was a great company.

* * *

Two contrasting cultures, one from the Welsh valleys, the other from the sun-parched plains of central Spain, came together in the year 2000 in the administrative offices of former dictator General Francisco Franco in the heart of Madrid. The get-together, combining a split crew of Welsh and Spanish film techs, was for the making of the movie *One of the Hollywood Ten*, which recounted an ugly and shameful chapter in American history when right-wing Senator Joe

McCarthy rose up almost unopposed to take on the mantle of a 20th century inquisitor, given the power to hunt down and arraign anybody, mainly in the Hollywood community, who had ever had the barest contact with the American Communist Party.

McCarthy showed a relentless determination, but most others in the government lay low, turned a blind eye and allowed the witch-hunt to proceed. It resulted in the career demolition of many of Hollywood's most familiar names, mostly actors and writers. Humphrey Bogart, Lauren Bacall, Burl Ives, Elia Kazan, Sterling Hayden, Arthur Miller and Dalton Trumbo were among those called in to testify under oath to any early associations they might have had with the American Communist Party. Some, like Ives and Kazan, implicated members of the Hollywood community; others, like Bogart and Arthur Miller, told the Committee to go take a jump in a lake. Fortunately they both survived the mud slinging. Others didn't.

Herbert Biberman, who had directed a privately financed picture on the Spanish Civil War titled *Salt of the Earth*, and his actress wife Gail Sondergaard were well up on the list of those forced to appear before the House Un-American Activities Committee, facing what amounted to charges of treason. In *One of the Hollywood Ten*, Biberman was played, and imposingly, by Jeff Goldblum and Sondergaard by Greta Scacchi. Goldblum was very thin and very tall, indeed almost skeletal, and seemed to subsist solely on a diet of herbal teas and unleavened bread. This was pretty difficult in Madrid, where every second doorway led into a tapas bar where the rojas and platefuls of delicacies were ready and waiting.

The story centred around Biberman and one of his main adversaries, my character, the prosecutor Parnell Thomas. Unfortunately, the courtroom set was blisteringly hot. That, added to the high-voltage exchanges between Biberman and Thomas, had my voice in shreds inside two days. Now hardly able to speak, I included a line in Parnell Thomas' dialogue apologising to the court for the condition of his voice, caused by a sudden throat infection. Just to keep the film medic happy, I took down two glasses of raw eggs a day, plus pots of herbal tea – Jeff Goldblum happily acting as procurer and provider of the sachets. That, plus a supplementary visit or two to a nearby tapas bar, had me almost back in business within two days.

Herbert Biberman wasn't so fortunate. On the thinnest of evidence he was found guilty of contempt of Congress and hardly worked again. Senator Joe McCarthy, who had instigated the anti-Communist witch-hunts mainly to bolster his chances for re-election to the Senate, died within a year of the close-down of the hearings from cancer. So endeth a lesson.

$\star \star \star$

Spy Game was my first outing for my new agents Emptage Hallett and my second with director Tony Scott. My first time was back in a 1983 film on the 'undead' theme called *The Hunger*, headlining David Bowie, Catherine Deneuve and Susan Sarandon. Eighteen years later it was *Spy Game* with Brad Pitt as a captured CIA operative and Robert Redford as a retired agent quickly reactivated to get him out. It was a good pairing that took the investigation from the planning stage in London to a terrorist attack in North Africa and back again.

In *The Hunger* I'd been given the role of an estate agent trying to unload a dilapidated piece of property. In *Spy Game* Tony Scott gave me another chance to get the role right by casting me as a property developer, this time trying to hook Redford into purchasing a rather elegant but definitely over-priced flat in Chelsea. In neither film did I sell so much as one square inch of floor space – Redford preferred mountains.

One day we were waiting on set for a lighting change, and there was something I'd always wanted to find out about.

'Getting *The Legend of Bagger Vance* on screen must have taken some doing,' I said.

'It did – you enjoyed it?

'I'm a golfer – I loved it. And Will Smith as an Eastern mystic coach! You take chances!'

'It was worth it,' he replied.

There was another Rimmer in the works on this one, middle son Ben, who was on the film roster as location manager in both London and Morocco. One incident Ben will never forget, and probably neither will Tony Scott, involved getting a requested series of stills of a staged terrorist explosives attack just on the edge of Rabat. The request came from Morocco's King Hassan III for inclusion in his personal archives. There would only be one crack at getting the sequence right; everything for metres around would be flattened so there would be no possibility of a retake.

Every detail in the preparatory set-up for the blast was scrupulously attended to. Explosive packs were carefully set in place, while all civilians, vehicles, even cats and dogs were evacuated and replaced with mock figures and over-the-hill cars and trucks. The time for the detonation was signalled and, in a split second, all hell broke loose. A massive roar accompanied the first eruption of flames, and clouds of thick, black smoke followed, billowing skyward. The staged explosion was a fiery, colossal, screen-filling success – except for one thing. Nobody had remembered to tell the 'stills' cameraman to photograph it for the Royal Household. Enter son Ben, unofficially 'snapping' different angles and incidents of the scene that he thought might be of interest. He got the complete shattering sequence of the blast safely tucked away on his Leica, to be handed over later to Tony Scott and then to King Hassan.

Talking of Ben, our next family wedding celebration was a few hundred miles nearer home than the one that united him and Catherine in Dublin. In fact, it was at a country church just a five-minute walk from our own front door. Our youngest son Paul decided to divest himself of his 33-year-old bachelorhood and just how could he resist Jacky? After all, she's brightened his life and all of ours as well.

The union brought great pleasure to the family because, up to then, Paul had appeared quite content in the environs of open fields and the company of every form of wildlife, from hawks and kites to March hares. At the reception, held in the large and stunningly decorated hall by friends of the family, his brother and Best Man, Damian, addressed both newlyweds in a most moving speech. As the celebration neared its close, the Dance Band struck up a chord inviting all present to form a large circle around the hall. As they continued playing, Paul and Jacky walked around it, greeting and thanking each and every person present. Then, waving adieu, they skipped down the stone pathway leading to a waiting black-and-white vintage Bentley, which took them to their undisclosed Hertfordshire hotel destination. Tremendous!

Chapter Fifteen

The voice on the other end of the line was young and had a sort of sing-song cadence to it, hinting at somewhere far to the east. At first I thought it was some joker pulling a dialect, not really funny because I could hardly understand a word of it. Then I made out the words 'Abe Masariho, booker from Japan, you okay for next week?' – it all clicked nicely into place and so did I, on the dotted line.

Star Wars and *Thunderbirds* had for some time been major attractions on Rising Sun movie and television screens – both were well into the cult zone. I had heard that young Abe, who had started in the booking business thanks to ready support from his family, was now holding down second place where annual international convention dates around the Far East were concerned. Apparently the relationship with his family was a comfortable one and the yen were still flowing.

So, on with the show. Aside from myself, Abe had secured the appearance of Tony Dyson, the creator of the *Star Wars* 'pocket rocket' R2-D2. Some coup! Dyson had also found time to set up the SFX control systems for *Superman II*, *Dragonslayer* and *The Empire Strikes Back*. With that sort of CV he could run for Emperor himself. I was beginning to think we were in for a nice ride.

A few minutes later the phone rang again – another call from Abe – this time with a problem, a rather tricky one. His third celebrity guest had to drop out because of a family situation. Did I have some quick suggestion as to who could replace him?

'Abe, give me a call back in half an hour.'

Garrick Hagon, a fellow Canadian otherwise known as Biggs Darklighter from *Star Wars*, flashed across my mind. But if he didn't answer my ring, I didn't know where to go after that. He did.

'Hey, Garrick. Fancy some sushi this week?'

'Sure – where?'

'Abe just phoned from Tokyo – he'd like us to come out for a five-day convention starting Friday – looks good.'

He checked his diary, the page dates were open, we had ourselves a trip. But first I had to call Jerome Blake – Mas Amedda of *The Phantom Menace* – and thank him for recommending me to Abe in the first place.

The deal with Abe would be for Business Class return flights, plus five days in and around Tokyo with traditional restaurant stops and premium choices of saké thrown in. At the conventions there would be payment for autographing photos and whatever else the fans brought to the tables. Everything sounded great except for the mention of traditional Japanese restaurants, which inevitably meant raw fish specialities – a phobia I'd carried around for most of my life. I'd rather chomp on grilled beetles than have to swallow any part of a raw fish. I resolved to have a quick word with Abe to explain, if asked, the reason for turning down the speciality of the house was a run-in with a very unlikeable octopus and I hadn't been able to look at so much as a sardine ever since.

Garrick and I met up at the Japan Airlines checking-in desk; Tony Dyson would fly in from Malta where he was now living, lock stock and robots. And hopefully Abe would be in the vicinity to meet us on our arrival.

Our touchdown at Tokyo Airport was enjoyably uneventful, a good way to start; who wants an eventful one? Abe swooped in and picked us up in a deluxe seven-door Nissan station wagon, Garrick and I slung in our luggage and we were quickly into the thrust and parry of traffic bound for the city centre. Abe's driving was black magic, sometimes missing the sides of other vehicles by hardly more than a coat of paint. He pulled up to the hotel entrance and let us out – I glanced at the chassis, not a scratch anywhere. Unbelievable. We checked in at reception and in less than half an hour were seated in the hotel lounge across from Tony Dyson, who was wearing a tropical sand-toned suit and maroon shirt, looking the spitting image of the Goons' Michael Bentine – and he probably had an IQ at about the same astronomical level. It was a happy hour table, all except for Abe, who appeared a little distant; something was on his mind. Tony noticed it too and leaned over to me.

'Don't worry about it, it's a Japanese thing. He'll be okay.'

The first two days of the tour went predictably well, with the second highlighted by a visit from my Canadian godson Paul, son of my original Three Deuces partner. Paul the younger was now doing splendidly as a financial whizkid living in Tokyo with his Japanese wife Taeko and son Michael. It was a grand get-together.

The next day wasn't.

Garrick had received a phone call at the hotel from an agent he had formerly worked for in Tokyo. The message was brief: 'There's going to be trouble at your show today – look out!'

Who the hell were we going to notify? International Rescue?

For the first part of the convention gathering, nothing appeared out of the ordinary; if anything, the line-up of fans outnumbered those of the two previous days. Then suddenly, ominously, something happened to the atmosphere in the place. A number of leather-jacketed young men eased into the entranceways to the auditorium, while fans close by shifted slowly and made room for them. In the two long queues to the celebrity tables, gaps were starting to appear as other fans began to edge away from their places in line as the leather-jacketed bunch strolled through. I heard a whispered word from several of the fans.

'Yakuza!'

It was the name given to organised gangs under one central command – they were a breed you'd never want to deal with. They stayed around long enough to make sure the queues wouldn't be taken up again, then sauntered out.

We stayed on for the few brave fans left, signing photos and practically giving away the merchandise on the tables, not wanting to give the Yakuza the satisfaction of any kind of total victory. Then we packed up and got out of there, more shaken than stirred, just as a squad of Tokyo police came in through the main entrance.

There was a message waiting for me back at the hotel from a young Japanese friend, Hiroshi Yamachi, who had lodged with us while studying English in London, inviting me to dinner at a noted traditional Japanese restaurant. The raw fish thing was going to come up again, and I was going to have to face it like St George and the Dragon. We were shown into a beautiful bamboo-toned room with very low and generously spaced tables – but no chairs. Nobody else around the room seemed to have any either. Hiroshi eased himself down on a tableside cushion and, smiling, gestured me to do the same. As I sat down my feet were dangling in a sizable pit under the table.

'We still hold on to some very traditional customs here in Japan,' he said with a smile. I nodded politely, which you seem to do a lot of in Japan. 'Your English is most impressive from the last time we talked,' I replied.

So, one problem sorted, but the waiter was now approaching with another – two starter dishes of raw tuna. All I could do was stare at my plate and the one visible eye looking back at me. But as my feet shifted around this underground bunker and I became aware of the depth of it, an idea began to form slowly in mind, my only way out. I sliced off a small chunk of the tuna from my dish and, tensing my stomach, swallowed it, just as a phone was brought to the table with a call for Hiroshi. I could feel the tuna working its way down to wherever it was headed and knew I just couldn't handle another piece. As Hiroshi excused himself and turned to take his call, I inched the plate of fish to the edge of the table and upended its contents into the pit, hoping the next person to sit on my cushion wasn't longer in the leg than I was and the restaurant would forgive my trespass. But what ensued was such a feeling of relief that I could hardly stop talking – and then neither could Hiroshi.

It was a great get-together, east and west, past and present...

For thousands of years, snow-capped Mount Fuji has been drawing pilgrims from every quarter of the world. It has been photographed countless times, written about probably even more, but from the distance of our foothills hotel, the venue for our final convention, with the mountain kilometres away, nothing quite prepares you for actually sighting it the first time. You don't just see it, you feel it. And that seems entirely appropriate for one of the natural glories of our world. Thanks for the trip, Abe.

★ ★ ★

It has a span of over 1,600 feet, a weight topping 5,000 tons, structured mainly in steel tangents and anchored granite, and a network of inter-linking cables, corded hawser lines and arches that at times give it the appearance of a giant, galactic spider's web. Sinatra has sung about it, Walt Whitman heaped poetic praises on it, and any northern state politician worth his gilt-edged bonds has been driven in a motorcade across it. It links the workaday, multi-layered street life of downtown Brooklyn to the glittering skyline of Manhattan over the deep-flowing East River. Completed in 1883, it was heralded immediately as one of the Seven Industrial Wonders of the World. It still is. It's called the Brooklyn Bridge.

Memories of the bridge and the time I had spent around it resurfaced in 2003 with an offer from BBC Worldwide to play the main 19th century financier of the project, William Kingsley. He secured the necessary funds to allow the construction to go ahead, but the final cost, unfortunately, far exceeded the monetary one. The death toll of those working under the waters of the East River rose to a number that almost halted the work before the bridge was anywhere near completion. Included in the toll was the man whose vision initiated the grand design of the construction, John Roebling (played by Steven Berkoff). After his death, a harrowing one, the project was taken over by his son Washington.

I remembered the bridge and the 45-minute walk across it from a long time back, following The Three Deuces' appearance at New York's Paramount Theatre. I'd hung on in New York after hearing through the actor's grapevine of a teacher who held slightly offbeat but rewarding acting classes in the heart of Manhattan. It was one of those things that keep tugging at you until you do something about it. I'd found a cold-water flat in the vicinity of Flatbush Avenue on the Brooklyn side, moved in a few things and prayed for a warm spell or at least a quilt.

Brooklyn is Brooklyn and there's really no other way to describe it. One of the first things you discover is that Brooklynese is not an accent, it's really another language. Seems that somewhere in its linguistic development the sound 'er' came to be pronounced as 'oy' and vice versa. If you were trying to locate the whereabouts of an oyster bar at Thirty-third Street and Third Avenue, you could ask all day and nobody would be able to understand what you were talking about. To have any hope of finding the place, you'd have to describe it as being an 'erster bar' at Toity-toid Street and Toid Avenoo. But once there, the oysters would be as delectable as you've tasted anywhere and the owner would probably bring over a half dozen more on the house, just for being able to find it.

Outside, and a turn to the left out of our 'erster' haven, lay a whole neighbourhood network of streets and avenues, chock full of sights, sounds and smells occupying the air from everywhere. For five blocks or so it was filled with the rapid swirls and crescendos of Italiano; a few streets further on you entered the gentler world of Jewish textile shops and delicatessens; across two more intersections and bearing right towards the river you were into Polish, then

Russian, though I was forever getting the two confused. Back to the left and it was the turn of the guttural sounds of German. After a time, I was told, every dweller got used to the facts of living in this sprawl of loosely defined precincts and nobody seemed to get in the way of anybody else. The place was a teeming delight.

But much as I loved it, most of where I wanted to get to was across the Hudson River and into Manhattan – the theatres, galleries and especially Carnegie Hall. Carnegie Hall was also, on the third floor, the studios of drama coach Betty Cashman. She was a lawyer and many said a brilliant one. During her career of some years in front of the New York Bar, she came to the conclusion that 'body language' as part of a lawyer's or an actor's bag is every bit as important as voice, sound or appearance. It could either add to or detract from the point being made. She began to attract a coterie of main-line lawyers to her studios, convinced of the importance of what she was teaching. Actors dropped in for refresher courses and under the Cashman eye began to take stock of how they were doing things for the first time in years.

It wasn't exactly the Actors Studio or the American Theatre Wing, but it had its own special attraction. The first was the dynamic Betty Cashman herself, and on my first night I met three others – Jack Palance, Zsa Zsa Gabor and Sammy Davis Jr. Palance, such a menacing presence on screen, was the gentlest of men, Zsa Zsa was delightfully kooky and Sammy Davis had a stock of stories that could see you through till dawn's early light and then wrap it up with a buck-and-wing tap dance that had you yelling for more.

It would be hard to imagine the three of them working the same picture, but at the studio they all pitched in, working with everybody, taking part in read-throughs, stressing the need for an actor to find himself a raison d'être and marking the right moment to 'wait' for the most striking effect. Palance even won a mock trial verdict over one of New York's big-name lawyers at a studio get-together that sent us howling joyfully out into the night. It was all tremendously vital and practical, everything raised in the class was worked on and explored. We were 'on the town' and New York's a different kind of town when you connect like that.

But back to Brooklyn. Over 100 years after its completion, the Brooklyn Bridge is still one of the most heavily used arterial routes into the island of Manhattan. The BBC's *Seven Wonders of the Industrial World* drama-documentary celebrating that achievement has now been shown everywhere around the world. It struck a universal chord and still does.

★ ★ ★

The two of us were standing on the high-altitude shoreline of Lake Wakaputi, well up in the mountains overlooking New Zealand's southern tip at Queenstown. Barry Authors, a long-time friend, now a writer and film producer, had brought me half way around the world to appear in a picture of his to be shot here. I could hardly take my eyes away from the array of wonders that surrounded us from every side.

'Sure as hell beats Scunthorpe on a Tuesday afternoon,' I said.

'There's a lot more.' Barry picked up a pebble from the sand and skipped it out across the water. 'How far do you figure it is to the other side?'

Not all that far, I thought. 'A mile, maybe a little more.'

'From here across there it's five miles at least, you can see forever.'

Unbelievable. But then, so were many things about this island.

Cloud-crested mountains, a succession of lakes and forests ranging out forever, and a year-round glacier – just the kind of terrain Barry wanted for a family adventure picture now into its third week, *Mee-Shee: The Water Giant*. The story and the prospective film had already gathered an encouraging amount of column space, mainly in North America under its original title *Ogo Pogo*. It was the name given by an Indian tribe from western Canada to a mythical underwater creature that lived in the depths of a lake owned and much revered by the tribe's ancestors for hundreds of years. The Indians at first agreed to the picture being made there and everything seemed about to roll. Then at a final pow-wow of the tribal elders, the agreement was rescinded. Barry Authors had the script, the cast and suddenly no location to shoot it in. The tribe was adamant. But so was Authors that the film was going to be made – elsewhere, if needs be – while interest was still warm.

After a swift revamping they found their new location, thousands of miles away, well below the Equator, in fact on the last outcropping of land before the coast of the Antarctic. It was exactly what Barry wanted, a great range of country filled with waterfalls, gorges, staggeringly beautiful scenery and a lake of inestimable depth. He had the place – New Zealand's South Island.

First on board after the financial backing had been secured was The Jim Henson Company, that had shot to the top of the animatronics field since the huge success of their TV series *The Muppet Show*, which was shown on every major television circuit around the world. Their brief on this one was to come up with a massive, terrifyingly authentic sea creature with a nature that turned out as playful as a trained seal's. The creature's new name, in deference to Canada's west coast Indians, would be Mee-Shee. If we'd landed just a few months before, there wouldn't have been a technician or a spare Klieg light available anywhere. Peter Jackson's *The Lord of the Rings* trilogy had scooped up everything and everybody around Queenstown, including half the Maori population as 'extras'.

They were two weeks into filming by the time I arrived on the last leg of my trip from Hong Kong. An eye-catching sight, coming in over the sea to Auckland, were the rows of gleaming hulls, spars and after decks of one of the most amazing gatherings of ocean-going luxury craft probably ever tied down in one harbour. They had sailed in from every point on the globe for the Around the World Yacht Race. The starting gun would fire the next day.

By then I had flown down to Queenstown to my first location posting as the Security Chief of an extensive and largely unspoiled waterside area on the outskirts of town. On the far side of the lake a high range of mountains looked staggeringly close, but I was learning to gauge distances a little better now; they were probably at least ten miles away. The director John Henderson and lead actor Bruce Greenwood, who had recently turned in such a mesmerising performance as President John F Kennedy in the film *Thirteen Days*, were huddled over the script as I approached them along the wharf. John Henderson, whom I'd certainly heard about but not met until now, looked across at me over Bruce's shoulder.

'Well, the long arm of the law! Welcome to the end of the world, Shane.'

I smiled back. 'Doesn't look that bad.'

Bruce Greenwood came over, hand outstretched. 'Far from it,' he said. 'The place is a treat, nice to see you.'

Greenwood was playing the father of a ten-year-old boy who forms a storybook friendship with the giant undersea creature Mee-Shee, a creature that in the eyes of an international oil development company presents a distinct threat to their undersea explorations in the area. A frustrated head office directive orders him to be eliminated at any cost, but Mee-Shee continues to elude every attempt by the conglomerate to carry out his annihilation. The boy, his father and the local Maori populace then link up, outsmart the company and force them to haul up anchor and beat a retreat.

Coming out of a history of family TV and film adventures, I felt quite at home with the whole scenario. But, as beautiful as the country was, it didn't make for the easiest of location shoots. There was a lot of muscle power needed on many of the uphill hikes – slippages at these kinds of heights could be costly, if not downright injurious to the health.

If you're looking for it, you can always find something to grumble about on a picture – but it's usually something personal and a bit selfish. On *Mee-Shee*, thanks mainly to the man in charge, there wasn't a trace of it above or below the water line. A feather in your cap, Mr Authors – and thanks for keeping me near ground level.

Meanwhile, the rather medium-paced Queenstown had been suddenly transformed into a backpackers Mecca, with *Lord of the Rings* fans from everywhere seeking out the hills, grottos and valleys where Gandalf the Grey worked his wizardry and the rest of the cast did their best to dodge it. The town merchants were of course delighted with the non-stop ringing of their cash registers due to the new influx of tourists, but a number of long-time residents were not all that crazy about having to suddenly line up for everything from the fish and chip shop to the District Assay office, where they dropped in to cash their gold panning takings from the rivers around town.

However, the general lift to the Queenstown economy and the mostly considerate behaviour of the backpackers dispersed a lot of that bad feeling and the citizens later concluded that the young travellers weren't such a bad bunch after all. The town even waived all bunji jump admission prices for them at the local gorge.

★ ★ ★

When travelling west across the Midland counties of England on the A428 towards Bedford, your eyes will suddenly be caught by the sight of two massively constructed buildings rising side by side, with little around them but gently rolling Bedfordshire farmland. Each appears big enough to house at least a hyper-market or two, but that's far from the purpose they were built for.

The time was the early 1940s during the mid stages of the Second World War, when London was under attack from repeated and devastatingly ruinous bombing raids by the German Luftwaffe under the command of Field Marshal Hermann Goring, whose announced aim was the utter destruction of British morale and the City of London along with it. The RAF, undermanned and flying patched-up Hurricane and Spitfire fighters at best, was finding it hard to stem the tide. Along with ground artillery fire, they formed the last line of defence. Something else was needed and it became top priority.

A British think tank got to work and came up with the idea of dirigibles – small and medium-sized airships, a lot of them – to be positioned in the midst of the attack corridors used by the incoming German bombers. If the strategy worked, the airship fleet would unhinge the bombers' navigational projections, obscure many of their target points and make the invaders easier prey for the British ground and air defences. It would also provide a breathing space for the emergency rebuilding of the RAF fighter force and allow a vital respite for the young men who piloted them. Swing-shift crews were quickly brought in and around-the-clock construction began, with the enormous hangars literally being built around them.

The dirigibles began appearing over the skies of London in an astonishingly short space of time, and the strategy to disrupt the blanket bombing worked to near perfection. The German pilots and navigators were thrown into confusion, the Luftwaffe lost its aerial authority and the Battle of Britain slowly but irrevocably changed the course of the war.

In 2004, after years of being more or less forgotten about, the fate of the two wartime hangars was about to take an unexpected twist. The *Batman* production juggernaut had landed in the UK determined to reverse its latest run of diminishing returns in the world's cinemas. The first item on the rehab agenda was to cut out a further continuation of Batman adventures and get back to the roots of the Batman story; in other words, produce a prequel. In one move they could delete the last over-the-top showings, sound a new, more serious and interesting note, wipe away the high gloss and get real. They mapped out the bones of the story, brought in Christopher Nolan (who had just sprinkled a little stardust on his career by directing the Al Pacino-Robin Williams thriller *Insomnia*), and

Batman Begins was up and flying.

While getting to work on the storyline, Nolan contracted Christian Bale (still skeletal from his latest cult film *The Mechanic*) for the new Batman and then added more flesh to the bones of the script in the persons of Liam Neeson and Michael Caine. Our son Ben was hired as location manager and the first brief handed him was to locate a large enough interior sound stage to film a colossal sequence of explosive special effects.

Ben remembered the two massive dirigible hangars standing almost unused close to the city of Bedford. It was a long shot, but the kind of challenge Ben rather liked. He found the present owners, offered them a contract that immediately lifted them out of the doldrums, and brought it back to Chris Nolan, who okayed it on the spot. It was a done deal. A little later in the week, over a late-night dinner and planning meeting, Chris suddenly asked Ben if he was related to the actor who had voiced his favourite *Thunderbirds* character, Scott Tracy, and Ben replied, 'Sure, he's my father!'

Chris let out a whoop – he had been a diehard fan of *Thunderbirds* all through his childhood – so Scott Tracy just had to be in the film! Next day I was offered the part of Gotham City's fractious Water Commissioner, who was in charge of turning back the course of a city-wide flood disaster. How NYC and Batman managed to survive the threat, only God and Supremo Nolan knew. It was also the first time that three Rimmers appeared on the credit list together, as by now Paul had graduated to an assistant location manager and transport organiser.

Chapter Sixteen

The year was 2005, the time late July, the place Tampa Florida – home of the NFL's Tampa Bay Buccaneers and also the Crown Plaza Hotel, venue for the 30th anniversary celebration of *Space: 1999* – 'Earthbound'. The welcome flags were up and waving in the Bay breeze for the arriving Spacers coming in from north, east and west. We'd flown in down Florida's east coast, past Jacksonville and Daytona Beach, then taken a swerve westward, immediately over the NASA Space Flight HQ at Cape Kennedy, towards our set-down destination at Orlando Airport. From there a car ride along the coast would take us the rest of the way into Tampa.

We were met at the arrivals gate by a tall, lightly bearded man standing head and shoulders above everybody else, dressed in a lumberjack's blue-checked shirt. He might have just loped down from a close-by mountain. His name was Michael Lindow, a gentle giant of a man and husband of Ellen, the organiser of the *Space: 1999* convention. He led us outside to a parked ten-year-old Mustang and seconds later, after a staccato burst of acceleration, had us speeding along the Interstate 75 under a cloudless blue sky, taking in lungfuls of the most beautifully rejuvenating coastal air. It was absolute bliss after inhaling eight hours of recycled 747 cabin ventilation on the way over, which had all the invigorating properties of a stick of candy floss.

Florida seemed like the promised land.

From the wind-swept back seat we snatched glimpses of the

rolling waters of the bay in between stretches of condominium build-ups that resembled huge cereal boxes upended along the beach. Such a crazy place of contrasts, I thought. Open air, exhilarating, vast stretches of sky blue water, almost impossibly beautiful in places – yet many of the inhabitants were penning themselves up in these terribly ugly urban high-rises.

We turned left at the next crossroads leading to the host hotel. A mile on was a large, sprawling, high-hedged building sign-boarded as Brandon Hospital, which boasted one of the leading cardiac clinics in the whole Tampa Bay area. We didn't take much notice of it on the way except that it seemed to take an awfully long time in getting from one end of it to the other.

Finally, through the towering doors of the convention hotel and to a reception desk that curved away almost out of sight, partly due to a spreading palm tree growing up in the middle of it. We ducked a few fronds and signed in. Our room was up on the second floor, conveniently close to the ice dispenser and just down the corridor from where our convention would be held. I say 'our' because there seemed to be two others going on – one with a room full of wide-eyed teeny boppers with nary a warden or a chaperone in sight, the other a crowd of white-striped revellers getting in some war dance rehearsals along the corridor. We were in for some kind of weekend.

The top celebrity for the *Space: 1999* convention was Barry Morse, the eccentric scientific boffin from Moonbase Alpha and in another world the obsessive tracker of David Janssen through numerous episodes of *The Fugitive,* one of the most watched television thrillers of all time. He had a fund of stories from a theatrical lifetime which easily took care of the entire two days of the get-together.

On the third day of our stay, four of us decided to leave him to it and drive out for a light lunch before the evening's grand finale. It was a nice idea but I didn't quite make it. The pains in my chest and upper right arm started shortly after leaving the hotel. Ellen phoned Michael back at their farm to seek advice and he immediately urged her to get me to the nearest hospital as quickly as possible. It happened to be the one we'd passed on the way in at Brandon.

It wasn't a serious heart attack, but it was certainly a warning shot over the ribcage. And it was enough to put me in a hospital bed until further explorations could be carried out. Ironically, the room they booked me into was light, attractive and certainly quieter than the one back at the hotel. Maybe, I thought, it wasn't going to be all that bad.

Next day I underwent a 'stent' procedure in which a tiny balloon is passed up through the artery which is constricting the blood-flow into the heart. The balloon is then inflated at the critical point, which opens up the blocked arterial area, restores the blood-flow and hopefully allows you to pass your very personal MOT. I really wasn't conscious of what was going on except that the surgeon, a slight, compact and perceptive young Indian man called Dr Khant, had a very calming effect on me. I do remember, though, holding out my hand to him before the operation, wishing us both good luck! After just three days, the inserted stents were deemed a success, which pleased Dr Khant and certainly tickled the hell out of me.

Thanks to the insurance coverage provided by Gold Card, organised by Sheila before we left, the cost of the operation plus drugs, plus a five-day recuperative stay in a ground-floor room overlooking the rear garden of the Tampa Holiday Inn, with rearranged airfares and an ambulance to meet us at Gatwick, was paid for without a murmur.

The Florida doctor's prescription had been to take it easy, free my mind of all concern and allow the body to recover itself. Well, for one of the few times in my life I did as ordered. Almost immediately I felt a faint but unmistakable itch to take a calm and clear look at the chain of past events – even better, to write them down. Those years from the 1950s to the 80s had been epic ones to have taken part in. They shouldn't just disappear.

But first, on a nearer horizon, there was an event at Pinewood

Studios to celebrate the 30th anniversary of – guess what? – *Space: 1999.* After an afternoon of screenings, talks, meeting old friends and one new one – Paolo Malaguti, the founder of the Italian Section of SHADO – we sat down to a mid-evening dinner with Gerry Anderson and the writer Chris Bentley, the chronicler of probably every step of Gerry's career.

The meal was excellent, the conversation flowed and it was good to be there. The trip homeward was another matter – chest tightening and a deeper pain following it. My cardiac bout that had started with the Tampa Bay medics had returned for another round. Without a word, Sheila changed direction and drove towards Barnet Hospital. Half an hour later, I was wheeled into the cardiac section with tubes and needles sticking out of me from all sorts of places. This time it was the real McCoy!

Ah, sweet mysteries of life.

I really only mention all this because it was the reason for missing the 'Countdown to Disaster' convention at the Borehamwood Hotel a few weeks later. Sheila came back from the convention with two bundles of cards wishing me well from everybody who attended the affair. You couldn't bottle the kind of tonic that came with those messages. Dr Yap, the normally laid-back head of the cardiac team, was deeply impressed with my recovery. So was I, when released from hospital a week before his forecast. It was a strange feeling being suddenly freed from a caring but closeted holding room – but beautiful, beautiful.

The first thing I did on returning home was sit in my favourite chair and raise a glass of vintage white. The next day I began to write. The book was to take me the best part of the next two years.

★ ★ ★

It was the most unlikely place to build a theatre, smack in the heart of a teeming, multi-cultural stretch of Kilburn High Street in north

London – on a site previously occupied by an auto repair garage. A long shout, too, from London's main theatre land in the West End. But shout they did, from the roof-tops, with a series of searingly controversial dramas. *Guantanamo, Justifying War, Nuremberg, Bloody Sunday* and, just to show they weren't totally immersed in the grittier side of life, John Buchan's *The 39 Steps*, which is still running in the West End.

The name of this surprisingly successful 300-seat showplace is the Tricycle Theatre, and its original stage productions have reached over 25 million people over the past 15 years. The creative force behind this cultural phenomenon is Nicolas Kent – unassuming maybe, but a most perceptive reader of theatrical potential, the national pulse, and a knowing motivator in placing before the public what they really want.

The production he had asked to see me about in 2007 was *Called to Account*, a staged court enquiry into whether Prime Minister Tony Blair should be brought to trial for 'the crime of aggression against Iraq'. Provocative stuff, but much of the Tricycle's stage fare was exactly that. After a very brief read-through at the theatre I was given the part of the American neo-con presidential advisor Richard Perle, an unofficial but powerful contributor to American international policy. He was often referred to as the Prince of Darkness. Bela Lugosi would have shone in the role.

Me, I was taken by the assured presence of the man, but repelled by his political stance. I had met him first through a recorded enquiry session and later when he flew over from Washington to see the play at the Tricycle. The cast was told not to inform me of his presence in the theatre in case I buckled at the knees half way through and made a spectacle of myself and the play.

I was called down to the theatre bar at the end of the play and there he was. He was as fluent and charming as a man in his slightly covert position had to be. He'd learned his trade well, even bought us both a large glass of Sauvignon Blanc and said he very much approved of the fairness in my playing of his character. He had been a student at the London School of Economics in his post American university days and later, as a respite from the tempestuous dog eat dog activities in Washington politics, had acquired a get-away place in the south of France, far enough away from most of the slings and arrows. To my surprise, it ended up a most comfortably spent evening.

But there was one cautionary note sounded. Any actor portraying a real, living character must not at any time add or alter one word that wasn't actually uttered in the recorded testimony and that was unconditional. A clear enough direction, but not always remembered once the battle between witness, prosecution and the defence began heating up. It was quite an assembly of political power players we were acting out and the cost of misrepresenting any one of them could come in at a staggeringly high price in a proper court of law. It came uncomfortably close a time or two, mainly by yours truly. But once back in the proper lane, it settled into a great, living experience.

Half the joy of it was in the 'actuality' drama of the piece, the other was being in the company of such a fine body of actors who would rate in any theatre in or out of the West End. Fittingly, it played for much of its run to standing room only audiences.

Thanks, Nicolas.

★ ★ ★

It's quite an excursion ticket I've been handed – some of it travelling light with little more than on-board luggage, a hotel address in case the film's driver doesn't show up, and the dialogue to be learned by the next morning. But at other times it was with family, five seats filled with anticipation about wherever it was we were landing – that was the choicest way to travel.

Some of the filming stops were a joy, others maybe a little less so – such a variable feast. But wherever the table was set, you took it as it came – from bolting down a hot spiced samosa while diving for cover under a daily Masai Mara cloudburst, to joining a Swedish film crew near Stockholm for a freezing outdoor smorgasbord lunch where it was so cold you could hardly unclench your teeth, to an idyllic summer picnic with a combined Anglo-French film crew just outside Fountainbleau during a break in the shooting of *S*P*Y*S*, overseen by a cordon bleu Paris chef (insisted upon by le crew Français).

At the moment my Canadian passport lies on a bookshelf just to the right of the desk where I have been recalling all this. It's looking a little forlorn and wondering maybe when it will be pressed into service again. Courage, mon brave. The pages are inked with a procession of stamped entrance and exit okays from almost everywhere. Though creased and often smudged, in some cases almost indecipherable, they hold a host of reminiscences which, like good wine, grow only more memorable as the years go by.

And so, time marches on. While Paul holds down the security fort for the latest *Harry Potter* film location deep in Surrey, Ben has returned to Morocco on a Matt Damon picture and Damian, with his computer-graphics gear, is somewhere up a mountain in southern Spain on a Saatchi commercial shoot, for which he will also supply his magic to the post-production work.

I've been lucky, blessed with a wife and family that have provided everything, a family that has flowered beautifully with the welcome arrival of two daughters in law, Catherine and Jacky, and three gorgeous grandchildren – Ella, Hugo and Kit. All that and the companionship of friends and neighbours along the way, some of whom have remained a part of our lives, others who have briefly appeared and just as quickly disappeared, but gifted us with spirits much expanded by the meeting.

Whoops! There goes the phone.

'Prague? When? This weekend ... *Lovelorn* – sci-fi script ... Yep, I think I might be able to handle that. See you over there ... Thanks!'

I pick up my passport from the shelf, blow a little dust off the front cover and head for my wardrobe to pick out some passable apparel for the owner of a bar and grill out in the far reaches of space. Then from somewhere come the words of an old Al Jolson show-stopper.

There's a rainbow 'round my shoulder
And a sky of blue above …

I'll tell you something … It ain't over 'til it's over!

Appendix

Film Credits

TITLE	YEAR	ROLE	DIRECTOR
Flaming Frontier	1958	Running Bear	Sam Newfield
A Dangerous Age	1959	Husband	Sidney J Furie
Dr Strangelove	1964	Co-Pilot Ace	Stanley Kubrick
The Bedford Incident	1965	Sparks Naval Officer	James B Harris
Thunderbirds Are Go	1966	Scott Tracy (voice)	David Lane
You Only Live Twice	1967	Control Operator	Lewis Gilbert
The Dirty Dozen	1967	Car Pool Sergeant Brady	Robert Aldrich
Thunderbird 6	1968	Scott Tracy / Carter (voices)	David Lane
Diamonds Are Forever	1971	Security Chief Tom Shaw	Guy Hamilton
Scorpio	1973	Detective Reisen	Michael Winner
S*P*Y*S	1974	CIA agent Hestler	Irvin Kershner
Rollerball	1974	Dallas coach Ace Logan	Norman Jewison
The 'Human' Factor	1975	Joe Carter	Edward Dmytryk
Nasty Habits	1977	Officer	Michael Lindsay-Hogg
Star Wars	1977	Incom Engineer	George Lucas
The People That Time Forgot	1977	Pilot Hogan	Kevin Connor
The Spy Who Loved Me	1977	Captain Carter, *USS Wayne*	Lewis Gilbert
Twilight's Last Gleaming	1977	Colonel Franklin	Robert Aldrich
Julia	1977	Customs Official	Fred Zinneman
Silver Bears	1978	American Banker	Ivan Passer
Warlords of Atlantis	1978	Captain Mike Daniels	Kevin Connor
Hanover Street	1979	Colonel Ronald N Bart	Peter Hyams
Arabian Adventure	1979	Abu – rebel leader	Kevin Connor
The Fiendish Plot of Dr Fu Manchu	1980	J Edgar Hoover	Piers Haggard

Shane Rimmer

TITLE	YEAR	ROLE	DIRECTOR
Superman II	1980	NASA Base Control Chief	Richard Lester
The Dogs of War	1980	Dr Harry Oaks	John Irving
Priest of Love	1981	John Kelly	Christopher Miles
Reds	1981	Chairman MacAlpine	Warren Beatty
Gandhi	1982	Edmund R Murrow	Richard Attenborough
The Hunger	1983	Arthur Jelinek	Tony Scott
Superman III	1983	Sheriff Mullins	Richard Lester
The Lonely Lady	1983	Adolph Fannon	Peter Sasdy
Morons from Outer Space	1985	Redneck Melvin	Mel Smith
The Holcroft Covenant	1985	NYPD Lieutenant Miles	John Frankenheimer
Dreamchild	1985	Studio Head Newman	Gavin Millar
White Nights	1985	Ambassador Jim Smith	Taylor Hackford
Out of Africa	1985	Gamekeeper Belnap	Sydney Pollack
Whoops Apocalypse	1986	Secretary of State Marvin Gelber	Tom Bussman
Crusoe	1988	Captain Mather	Caleb Deschanel
A Kiss Before Dying	1991	Commissioner Malley	James Dearden
Company Business	1991	Chairman, Maxine Gray Cosmetics	Nicholas Meyer
Year of the Comet	1992	Executive T T Kelleher	Peter Yates
Chaplin	1992	Manager / Agent	Richard Attenborough
Piccolo, Grand Amore	1993	Mr Hughes	Carlo Vanzina
A Kid in King Arthur's Court	1995	Baseball Coach	Michael Gottlieb
Space Truckers	1996	E J Saggs	Stuart Gordon
One of the Hollywood Ten	2000	Prosecutor J Parnell Thomas	Karl Francis
Spy Game	2001	Estate Agent Reg Bowels	Tony Scott
Batman Begins	2005	Lennie, Gotham Water Board Technician	Christopher Nolan
Mee-Shee: The Water Giant	2005	Bob Anderson	John Henderson
Alien Autopsy	2005	Colonel	Jonny Campbell
Lovelorn	2009	The Barman	Becky Preston

(Films listed by date of release)

TV Film Credits

TITLE	YEAR	ROLE	DIRECTOR
Baffled!	1973	Track Announcer	Philip Leacock
Charlie Muffin	1979	CIA Agent Braley	Jack Gold
Very Like a Whale	1981	Commuter	Alan Bridges
Nairobi Affair	1984	Jason Gardner	Marvin J Chomsky
Gulag	1985	Jay Bradley	Taylor Hackford
Reunion at Fairborough	1985	Joe Szylik	Herbert Wise
The Last Days of Patton	1986	Dr Colonel Lawrence Ball	Delbert Mann
Of Pure Blood	1986	Colonel Kranz	Joseph Sargent
Anastasia: The Mystery of Anna	1986	Harvey Coward	Marvin J Chomsky
The Return of Sherlock Holmes	1987	Stark	Kevin Connor
The Two Mrs Grenvilles	1987	Doorman	John Erman
Riviera	1987	Doc Ed Turner	John Frankeheimer
Roman Holiday	1987	Editor Hogan	Noel Nosseck
The Bourne Identity	1987	General Alexander Conklin	Roger Young
Tailspin: Behind the Korean Airliner Tragedy	1988	Admiral Riley	David Darlow
Red King, White Knight	1989	General	Geoff Murphy
Double Vision	1991	Twins' Father	Robert Knights
Only Love	1998	Warren Oliver	John Erman
Dockers	1999	US Longshoreman	Bill Anderson
Caught in the Act	2004	George, the Father	Jeffrey Reiner
Hiroshima	2005	US Secretary of State James F Byrnes	Paul Wilmshurst

(Films listed by date of original broadcast)

Television Credits

TITLE	YEAR	EPISODE	ROLE
Come Fly with Me	1958	(13 episodes)	Host/Singer
Armchair Theatre	1959	*Star in the Summer Night*	Paul
After Hours	1959	(4 episodes)	Vocal Singer
Armchair Theatre	1959	*Roast Goose and Walnut Stuffing*	Campbell
RCMP	1960	*Day of Reckoning*	Tom Hopwood
Compact	1963	(bi-weekly soap)	Editor Russell Corrigan
The Saint	1964	*The Hi-Jackers*	Major Smith
Theatre 625	1964	*Parade's End: A Man Could Stand Up*	
			Corporal Girtin
Thunderbirds	1965	(32 episodes)	Scott Tracy (voice)
		Trapped in the Sky	TX 204 Co-Pilot (voice)
		Pit of Peril	Johnny (voice)
		Terror in New York City	Scanners / Washington (voices)
Danger Man	1965	*The Mercenaries*	Buchanan
Thunderbirds	1965	*Operation Crash-Dive*	Radar Operator (voice)
		Vault of Death	Carter (voice)
		The Mighty Atom	Control Assistant (voice)
Thirty-Minute Theatre	1966	*The Flipside*	Bud Burdine
Thunderbirds	1966	*Martian Invasion*	Film Crewman (voice)
Play of the Month	1966	*Lee Oswald: Assassin*	Marine Sergeant
Doctor Who	1966	*The Gunfighters* (serial)	Seth Harper
Court Martial	1966	*All Roads Lead to Callaghan*	Ramsey
Orlando	1966	(6 episodes)	Kahn
Captain Scarlet and the Mysterons			
	1967	*Special Assignment*	Mason (voice)
	1968	*Inferno*	Pilot (voice)
		Flight to Atlantica	Sergeant (voice)
Coronation Street	1968	(bi-weekly soap)	Sergeant Joe Donelli
Joe 90	1968	*Most Special Astronaut*	Kent (voice)
		International Concerto	Kelly / Clark / Technician (voices)
		Big Fish	Gardner (voice)
		Business Holiday	Colonel Henderson / Taxi Driver (voices)
	1969	*Double Agent*	Radio Control (voice)

TITLE	YEAR	EPISODE	ROLE
UFO	1970	*Identified*	Lieutenant Bill Johnson
		Computer Affair	Lieutenant Bill Johnson
On Trial	1970	*The Chicago Conspiracy Trial*	Thomas Foran
UFO	1971	*Confetti Check A-OK*	CIA Agent Rosen
The Persuaders!	1972	*Element of Risk*	Lomax
The Protectors	1973	*Vocal*	Vickers
The Investigator	1973	(unscreened pilot)	John (voice)
Orson Welles Great Mysteries			
	1973	*In the Confessional*	Police Sergeant Warren
The Protectors	1974	*Zeke's Blues*	Zeke Daley
QB VII	1974	(mini-series)	Reporter
Late Night Drama	1974	*I Know What I Meant*	Ronald Ziegler
You're On Your Own	1975	*Value for Money*	Peter Kovacs
Space: 1999	1975	*Breakaway*	Eagle Pilot (voice)
Quiller	1975	*Thundersky*	Harry Brent
Space: 1999	1975	*Matter of Life and Death*	Bannion (voice)
Horizon	1976	*Billion Dollar Bubble*	Fred Levin
Space: 1999	1976	*Space Brain*	Kelly
		The Testament of Arkadia	Operative (voice)
		The Last Enemy	Eagle Pilot (voice)
Hadleigh	1976	*Divorce*	Pollack
Second Verdict	1976	*The Lindbergh Kidnapping*	Harold Giles Hoffman
Space: 1999	1976	*The Lambda Factor*	Technician (voice)
Alternative 3	1977		Bob 'Buzz' Grodin
Play of the Week	1977	*Professional Foul*	Stone
The Standard	1978	*Two Birds, One Stone*	Jack Putnam
The Famous Five	1978	*Five on Finniston Farm*	Mr Henning
The One and Only Phyllis Dixey			
	1978		US Colonel
Power Struggle	1978		Milton Shaw
Return of the Saint	1979	*Dragonseed*	Falco
A Man Called Intrepid	1979	(mini-series)	Willoughby
Secret Army	1979	*The Execution*	Canadian Commandant
BBC2 Playhouse	1979	*Speed King*	Ambassador Bingham
Tales of the Unexpected	1980	*My Lady Love, My Dove*	Arthur Beauchamp
Oppenheimer	1980	(serial)	Ed Condon
Bognor	1981	*Let Sleeping Dogs Lie* (serial)	Horace Higgins
The Rose Medallion	1981	(mini-series)	Sergeant Ed Kusborski

Shane Rimmer

TITLE	YEAR	EPISODE	ROLE
Nanny	1982	*Fathers*	Dick Leonard
Tales of the Unexpected	1982	*Man With a Fortune*	John Smith
Philip Marlowe, Private Eye			
	1983	*Smart Aleck Kill*	Detective Murphy
Agatha Christie's Partners in Crime			
	1983	*The Crackler*	Hank Ryder
Alas Smith & Jones	1984	(3 episodes)	(various sketches)
Master of the Game	1984	(mini-series)	Hugh Carroll
Lace	1984	(mini-series)	Hal Carson
Hammer House of Mystery and Suspense			
	1984	*Last Video and Testament*	Dr Hersh
Mistral's Daughter	1984	(mini-series)	Harry Klein
Ellis Island	1984	(mini-series)	TV announcer Duffy
Star Quality	1985	*Mr & Mrs Edgehill*	Brod Stanton
Space	1985	(mini-series)	General Quigley
Dick Spanner	1986	(22 episodes)	Dick Spanner (voice)
Space Police	1986	*Star Laws* (unscreened pilot)	Lieutenant Chuck Brogan
Breakthrough at Reykjavik			
	1987		George P Schultz
The Bretts	1988	*Home and Away: Part One*	Ben Silverstein
Dirty Dozen: The Series	1988	*Don Danko*	Agent Biddle
Mario Puzo's The Fortunate Pilgrim			
	1988	(mini-series)	Reilly
A Very British Coup	1988	(serial)	US Secretary of State
Coronation Street	1989	(episode 2852)	Malcolm Reid
The Saint	1989	*The Software Murders*	Bob Harrison
Street Legal	1989	*Basketball Story*	Detective Barnes
Fiendens Fiende	1990	*Del 4*	Skip Harrier
The Nightmare Years	1990	(mini-series)	Ambassador Dodd
Van der Valk	1991	*A Sudden Silence*	Lowell J Wallace
Stanley and the Women	1991	(mini-series)	Morton Fendig
Land of Hope and Gloria	1992	*The Authentic Taste of England*	Bob
Lipstick on Your Collar	1993	(serial)	Colonel 'Truck' Trekker
Ivar Kreuger	1998		President Hoover
Seven Wonders of the Industrial World			
	2003	*Brooklyn Bridge*	William Kingsley

(Programmes listed by date of original broadcast)

Theatre Credits

TITLE	YEAR	VENUE	DIRECTOR
Mary Mary	1964	Queen's Theatre, Hornchurch	David Perry
True West	1981	National Theatre	John Schlesinger
Guys and Dolls	1982	National Theatre	Richard Eyre
King	1990	Piccadilly Theatre, London	Graham Vick, Clark Peters
Arsenic and Old Lace	1993	Chichester Theatre	Annie Castledine
Death of a Salesman	1996	National Theatre	David Thacker
Of Thee I Sing	1998	Opera North, Leeds	Caroline Gawn
Called to Account	2007	Tricycle Theatre, London	Nicolas Kent

TV Scriptwriting Credits

TITLE	YEAR	EPISODE	DIRECTOR
Captain Scarlet and the Mysterons			
	1967	*Avalanche*	Brian Burgess
		Expo 2068	Leo Eaton
		Inferno (with Tony Barwick)	Alan Perry
Joe 90	1967	*Splashdown*	Leo Eaton
	1968	*Big Fish*	Leo Eaton
		Relative Danger	Peter Anderson
		King for a Day	Leo Eaton
		The Fortress	Leo Eaton
		Breakout	Leo Eaton
The Secret Service	1968	*Hole in One*	Brian Heard
The Protectors	1972	*Zeke's Blues*	Jeremy Summers
	1973	*Blockbuster*	Jeremy Summers
The Investigator	1973	(story for unscreened pilot)	Gerry Anderson

(Programmes listed by date of production)

Index

Picture Acknowledgements

Unless otherwise stated, all pictures are from the author's collection. We gratefully acknowledge the following additional sources:

Jacket front
The Spy Who Loved Me © Eon Productions/United Artists.
Thunderbirds © ITV Global Entertainment.

Jacket back
Portrait by John Vickers.

Back flap
Portrait by Ben Rimmer.

Frontispiece
Coronation Street © ITV Global Entertainment.

Picture section one
Page 1 and 2: *Come Fly With Me* © CBC.
Page 4: *Flaming Frontier* © Regal Films of Canada,
Dr Strangelove © Columbia Pictures, *Compact* © Radio Times.
Page 5: *Thunderbirds* © ITV Global Entertainment.
Page 6: *Doctor Who* © Eric Piper/Mirrorpix,
Coronation Street © John C Madden/ITV Global Entertainment,
UFO © ITV Global Entertainment.
Page 7: *The Protectors* © ITV Global Entertainment.
Page 8: *Rollerball* © Algonquin Films/United Artists.

Picture section two
Page 1: *Star Wars* © Lucasfilm/20th Century-Fox,
The Spy Who Loved Me © Eon Productions/United Artists.
Page 2: *Warlords of Atlantis* © Canal Plus Image (UK).
Page 3: *Arabian Adventure* © Canal Plus Image (UK),
Gandhi © Frank Connor/Columbia Pictures.
Page 4: *Tales of the Unexpected* © ITV Global Entertainment,
Out of Africa © Universal Pictures.
Page 5: *Dick Spanner* © Anderson Entertainment, *Daily Mirror* © Trinity Mirror.
Page 7: *Space Police* © Anderson Entertainment,
Lipstick On Your Collar © Whistling Gypsy Productions/Channel Four.
Page 8: top picture © Chris King.

Any errors or omissions will be corrected in future editions.